VISUAL QUICKSTART GUIDE

CorelDRAW 7

FOR WINDOWS 95/NT

Phyllis Davis

Peachpit Press

Visual QuickStart Guide
CorelDraw 7 for Windows 95/NT
Phyllis Davis

Peachpit Press
2414 Sixth Street
Berkeley, CA 94710
510-548-4393
800-283-9444
510-548-5991 (fax)

Find us on the World Wide Web at:
http://www.peachpit.com

Peachpit Press is a division of Addison Wesley Longman

Copyright © 1997 by Phyllis Davis

Cover design: The Visual Group
Interior design and production: Phyllis Davis

ISBN 0-201-69420-4

9 8 7 6 5 4 3 2

Printed and bound in the United States of America

This book is dedicated to my best friend,

HAROLD

Heartfelt thanks to

Nancy Davis, the best editor in the world.

and

Roslyn Bullas and Matt Wagner for their trust in me. Without them, this book would have never happened.

and

Kate Reber whose wise suggestions about layout and production helped make this book look so good.

Table of Contents

Table of Contents

Chapter 11   **Working with Text**   **133**

Table of Contents

Table of Contents

Table of Contents

The Basics

Welcome to the amazing world of CorelDraw 7! I am a professional user and big fan of CorelDraw, and have been for many years. This latest version knocks my socks off!

My purpose in writing this book is to share my experience as a professional who has worked extensively with CorelDraw. In keeping with the *Visual QuickStart Guide* format, my aim is to present easy, step-by-step directions with illustrations to take the mystery out of graphic design.

CorelDraw 7 offers a complete set of tools for creating many kinds of drawings and multi-page documents, from birthday cards, brochures, newsletters, and logos to precision blueprints and garden designs. This program has incredible power and loads of features, all incorporated into a newly-designed interface. As sophisticated as it is, it's also easy to use. You can run with it as far as you please. With CorelDraw 7 and your imagination, the sky's the limit! (And Corel ain't payin' me to say this!)

If you are new to CorelDraw 7, the program may seem a bit dense at first because it is so rich in features. But, if you take it one step at a time—putting one foot in front of the other down the road of graphic design— you'll be creating beautiful drawings in no time. For those of you who are acquainted with previous versions of CorelDraw, use this book as a guide to new features and techniques, and as a handy reference.

Happy drawing!

Introduction

WHAT IS CORELDRAW 7?

CorelDraw 7 is an *object-oriented* drawing program. Objects are created using drawing tools that make shapes defined by mathematical formulas. A CorelDraw object has properties that can be changed without affecting the way it looks close up or far away. You can move an object easily without affecting other objects around it.

Computer imaging programs are either based on *objects* or *bitmap* images. Other terms for object are *vector* or *drawing*; another term for bitmap is *raster*.

As with Windows 95, each object has properties. Hence, a vector object has properties that define it, such as color, shape, and size. A vector object appears the same on the screen with smooth lines and continuous colors, whether you are looking at it from far away or up close. Vector drawings are *resolution independent*, meaning that the printout quality depends only on the resolution of the printer.

Bitmap images are made up of tiny dots called *pixels* that are arranged and colored to form a pattern. The shape and color of a bitmap image appears smooth from a distance, but if you were to view a bitmap image close up, you would see tiny individual squares. Bitmap images depend on the resolution at which they are saved for printout quality.

In addition to its extensive and powerful vector drawing tools, CorelDraw 7 includes drawing management tools,

full-fledged writing tools, new bitmap capabilities, a user-friendly help system, and more than 32,000 pieces of clipart, and over 1,000 fonts.

WHAT'S NEW IN CORELDRAW 7?

There are so many new features that a complete list would be huge. Below are some of the new and enhanced features:

- Interactive Blend Tool—with this tool, you can just press and drag to create fast blends

- Interactive Fill Tool—using this tool, you can quickly add special fills to objects

- Internet tools—you can map images and add alternate text, save graphics and text in .Gif, .Jpg, and .Htm file formats, and more

- Panning Tool—using this tool, you can quickly move to any part of a drawing

- Property Bar—a context-sensitive toolbar that displays commands related to the selected object

- Spiral Tool—you can now create logarithmic spirals, varying the rate of a spiral's expansion

- Text Tool—with this one tool you can create both artistic and paragraph text, highlight text, fit text directly to an object's path, and enter text directly inside an object's shape

- Scrapbook—a new roll-up that lets you quickly access clipart

HOW DOES CORELDRAW 7 WORK?

CorelDraw documents are made up of separate elements called *objects*. An object's edge is called a *path*. Paths can be *closed* or *open*. An object with a closed path can be filled with color, whereas an object with an open path cannot. The path of an object passes through *nodes* that shape the path.

Some CorelDraw tools automatically create closed path objects. For instance, the Ellipse Tool makes various sized ovals and circles, the Rectangle Tool makes rectangles and squares, and the Polygon Tool makes polygons with any number of sides.

Other tools create closed or open path objects, depending on how they are used. The Freehand Tool can be used to draw a line (an open path) or a squiggly circle (a closed path). The Bézier Tool can be used to draw smooth curving lines, or closed, curvy shapes.

If you want to modify an object, you must first tell the program which object to modify by *selecting* it. When an object is selected, *handles* appear in a rectangular formation around the object.

Objects can be modified using a variety of features including menu commands, dialog boxes, *roll-ups*, and tools. For instance, an object's path can be shaped by moving its nodes and *control points* with the Shape Tool. An object can be *uniformly filled* with a *spot* or *process* color with one click using the Color Palette. Objects can also be filled with

patterns, textures, and *fountain fills* with the Interactive Fill Tool. Objects can be *rotated*, *skewed*, *scaled*, and *mirrored* using their handles and the Pick Tool. With the Blend roll-up you can blend one object into another, creating a morph.

CorelDraw lets you be creative with text. Text can be either *artistic* or *paragraph* and can float free on the page as a *text object*, follow the path of an object, or use an object as a container to shape it. Text can also be *converted to curves*, changing it to a graphical object whose outline can be modified like any other object's outline.

You can change the view of a drawing to make editing easier. You can *zoom in* to get a close up look and work with small details and *zoom out* to see the drawing as a whole. You can also use the Panning Tool to move the drawing in the drawing window.

To speed up screen redraw and help with editing, a document can be viewed in *simple wireframe, wireframe*, or *draft* mode. The drawing can also be seen in *enhanced* mode or *Full-Screen Preview*.

You can use precision tools such as *guidelines*, *grids*, *rulers*, and the *Align and Distribute roll-up* to make your drawings exact.

When you finish a drawing, your file can be *printed* or *saved to file* for *high resolution output* or as *separations*. You can see what the printed document will look like in *Print Preview mode*.

THE CORELDRAW 7 SCREEN (FIGURE 1)

1a Title Bar   **1b** Current Open   **2** Menu Bar   **3** Standard   **4** Property
Document   Toolbar   Bar

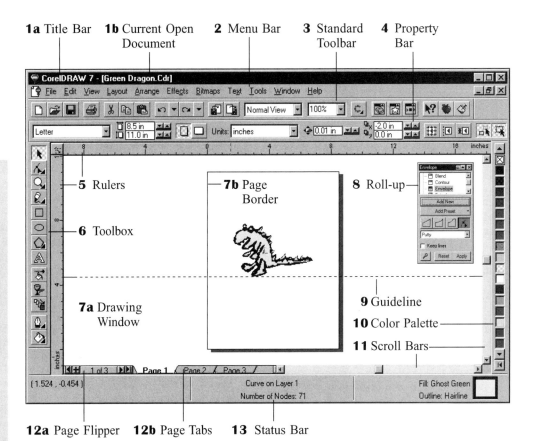

5 Rulers   **7b** Page   **8** Roll-up
                          Border

6 Toolbox

7a Drawing   **9** Guideline
Window   **10** Color Palette
                                              11 Scroll Bars

12a Page Flipper   **12b** Page Tabs   **13** Status Bar

KEY TO THE CORELDRAW 7 SCREEN

1a, b *Title Bar*
Displays the program name and current document name.

2 *Menu Bar*
Click any menu title to access commands, fly-outs, and dialog boxes.

3 *Standard Toolbar*
One of nine toolbars, the Standard Toolbar buttons give you quick access to standard Windows 95 commands such as New, Open, Save, Cut, Copy, Paste, and Print. It also includes several CorelDraw 7 commands, including Import, Export, View, and Zoom.

The CorelDraw 7 Screen

4 *Property Bar*

The Property Bar is a new CorelDraw 7 feature. It is a *context-sensitive* toolbar. Buttons and drop-down lists change dynamically, depending upon what is selected. This gives you easy access to the most important commands associated with the selected item.

5 *Rulers*

The mouse pointer's current position is indicated with marks on the vertical and horizontal rulers. Rulers can be moved to where you need them and used to accurately size objects. The measurement unit they display can be changed to virtually any system.

6 *Toolbox*

One of the nine toolbars, the Toolbox contains thirty-eight drawing and editing tools. As with every toolbar, you can drag it out onto the drawing window, making it float, or dock it along the edge of the screen, as shown here.

7a, b *Drawing Window* and *Page Border*

You can draw anywhere you want in the drawing window, but anything outside the page border will not be printed.

8 *Roll-up*

Roll-ups are like floating power tools on your desktop. There are 25 roll-ups, each geared to a specific command and its options, such as extrude, scale, mirror, blend, rotate, and envelope.

9 *Guidelines*

A non-printing guide that comes in three flavors—horizontal, vertical, and angled. Guidelines are used for aligning objects. Press and drag from either ruler to create guidelines.

10 *Color Palette*

The Color Palette is used to fill and outline your objects with color. There are thirteen defined color systems that can be loaded into the Color Palette, including Pantone, Trumatch, and Toyo.

11 *Scroll Bars*

Scroll Bars are used to navigate around the drawing window. If you click the down arrow on the vertical scroll bar, the drawing page will move up. If you click the right arrow on the horizontal scroll bar, the page will move left.

12a, b *Page Flipper* and *Page Tabs*

The page flipper is used to add pages to a document, and to move to another page, or to the beginning or end of a document. The page tabs give quick access to nearby pages.

13 *Status Bar*

Displays the position of the mouse pointer, and detailed object information, such as size, fill color, outline width, and position. Click the right mouse button on the Status Bar to access a pop-up menu you can use to select other information options.

The CorelDraw 7 Screen

CorelDraw 7 Controls *(sidebar)*

CorelDraw 7 controls

Figures 2a–f show the controls that you will use when working with CorelDraw 7 dialog boxes.

Figure 2a. *Text boxes and spin buttons. You can enter text or numbers in text boxes. Spin buttons are used to increase or decrease numbers. To increase a number, click the up arrow. To decrease a number, click the down arrow.*

Figure 2b. *Sliders let you increase or decrease a setting. To move the slider, position the mouse over the slider bar, press the left mouse button, and drag right to increase or left to decrease.*

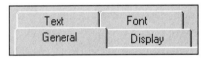

Figure 2c. *Found in dialog boxes, tab pages give access to commands and are organized by category. Click a tab to move from one tab page to another.*

Figure 2d. *Check boxes. Click a check box to turn an option on or off. A check in the box indicates that the option is on.*

Figure 2e. *Drop-down lists present a selection of items from which to choose. To open the list, click the little arrow to the right of the list box. Some drop-down lists allow you to enter your text.*

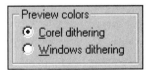

Figure 2f. *Option buttons. Option buttons are usually contained in an area, and you can select only one item from two or more options. Click the small circle to select an option. The selected option button has a black dot in it.*

Figure 3. *Click a menu title on the Menu Bar to open the menu.*

This arrow indicates a fly-out

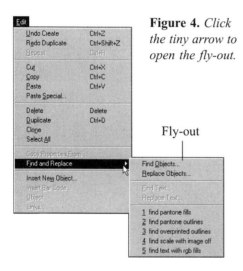

Figure 4. *Click the tiny arrow to open the fly-out.*

Fly-out

MENUS

There are 11 menus available on the Menu Bar. These menus give access to commands, fly-outs—sub-menus that open off of main menus—and dialog boxes.

To open a menu and select an item:

1. Position the mouse pointer over a menu title and click. The menu will open (**Figure 3**). If you see a tiny arrow to the right of a menu item, it means that there is an available fly-out. To open the fly-out, click the tiny arrow (**Figure 4**).

2. Move the mouse down to highlight the item you want.

3. Click to select the item.

Tip:

- A menu item with an ellipsis (...) after it means that this item will open a dialog box.

Menus; Terms Used in this Book

TERMS USED IN THIS BOOK

- *Click* means to quickly press and release the left mouse button.

- *Double-click* means to quickly press and release the left mouse button twice.

- *Right click* means to quickly press and release the right mouse button.

- *Select* or *choose* means to use the mouse pointer to highlight a menu item and click.

TOOLBARS

There are 9 toolbars available in CorelDraw 7. They give access to commands and dialog boxes with just the click of a button. Three toolbars are available, by default, when you launch CorelDraw 7 for the first time. They are the Standard Toolbar, the Property Bar, and the Toolbox.

To access the toolbars:

1. Choose ToolBars from the View menu (**Figure 5**). The Toolbars dialog box will open (**Figure 6**).

2. Click to place a check in the check boxes next to the toolbars you want to display.

3. Click OK. The toolbars you selected will appear.

Tip:

- All toolbars can be used *floating* or *docked*. An example of a docked toolbar is the Toolbox. In Figure 1 on page 4, the Toolbox is docked on the left side of the screen. To undock the Toolbox and make it float, position the mouse pointer over a gray area of the Toolbox not covered by a button. Press the left mouse button and drag the Toolbox to the right. To dock any toolbar, drag it to any edge of the screen—top, bottom, left, or right.

Figure 5. *Choose ToolBars from the View menu.*

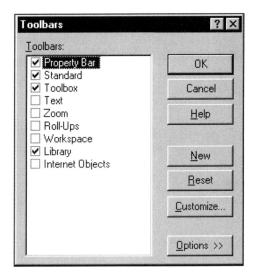

Figure 6. *Put checks in the check boxes next to the toolbars you want to have displayed, then click OK.*

THE TOOLBOX

The Toolbox (**Figure 7**) contains 38 tools used for creating and editing objects. Many of the tools are located on fly-outs, accessed by clicking the tiny black arrow at the lower-right corner of the tool button. The letters to the right of the Toolbox in Figure 7 indicate the corresponding fly-out (**Figures 8a–f**).

Figure 7. *The CorelDraw 7 Toolbox.*

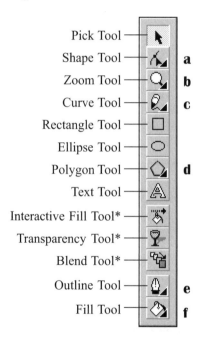

Pick Tool
Shape Tool — a
Zoom Tool — b
Curve Tool — c
Rectangle Tool
Ellipse Tool
Polygon Tool — d
Text Tool
Interactive Fill Tool*
Transparency Tool*
Blend Tool*
Outline Tool — e
Fill Tool — f

* A new CorelDraw 7
Interactive tool.

Figures 8a–f. *Toolbox fly-out menus.*

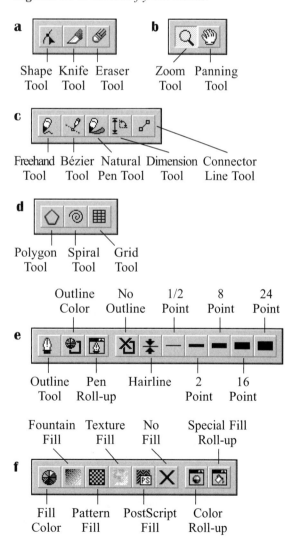

a — Shape Tool, Knife Tool, Eraser Tool

b — Zoom Tool, Panning Tool

c — Freehand Tool, Bézier Tool, Natural Pen Tool, Dimension Tool, Connector Line Tool

d — Polygon Tool, Spiral Tool, Grid Tool

e — Outline Color, No Outline, 1/2 Point, 8 Point, 24 Point, Outline Tool, Pen Roll-up, Hairline, 2 Point, 16 Point

f — Fountain Fill, Texture Fill, No Fill, Special Fill Roll-up, Fill Color, Pattern Fill, PostScript Fill, Color Roll-up

The Toolbox

THE PROPERTY BAR

The Property Bar (**Figure 9**), located by default near the top of the screen below the Standard Toolbar, is a context-sensitive command bar. It displays different buttons and options depending on which tool or object is selected. For instance, when the Zoom Tool is selected, the Property Bar contains only zoom-related commands.

Figure 9. *The Property Bar is context-sensitive. If nothing is selected, it displays tools that pertain to the overall document such as page size and orientation.*

THE STATUS BAR

The Status Bar (**Figure 10**) is your guide to what's happening in the drawing window. It gives you information about the position of the pointer and the properties of the selected object, including its shape, size, and fill and outline colors. You can change the information shown on the Status Bar by clicking the right mouse button on the bar and selecting different information options (**Figure 11**).

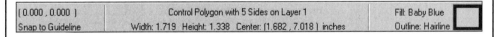

Figure 10. *The Status Bar shows you what's happening and gives information about what's selected.*

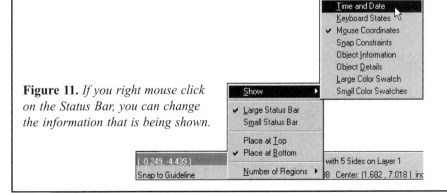

Figure 11. *If you right mouse click on the Status Bar, you can change the information that is being shown.*

Figure 12. *To select the Panning Tool, click the small arrow at the bottom right of the Zoom Tool, then select it from the fly-out.*

Figure 13. *Once you've selected the Panning Tool, it appears in the Toolbox. To get the Zoom Tool back in that position, just select it from the fly-out.*

A PANNING TIP

When you use the Panning Tool, you are only moving the drawing within the drawing window, not moving the drawing around on the actual page.

THE PANNING TOOL

The Panning Tool is used to move a drawing within the drawing window.

To use the Panning Tool:

1. Click the small arrow at the bottom right of the Zoom Tool to access the fly-out (**Figure 12**).

2. Click the Panning Tool to select it. Notice that the Panning Tool takes the place of the Zoom Tool in the Toolbox when it is selected (**Figure 13**). The mouse pointer will change to a hand.

3. Position the mouse over the drawing window.

4. Press the left mouse button and drag. The drawing will move within the drawing window.

KEYBOARD SHORTCUTS

Many menu commands have keyboard equivalents. Keyboard shortcuts (also called *hot keys*) always use the Ctrl, Shift, or Alt keys (or a combination of them) plus a letter or number key. Many times the letter is a mnemonic. For instance, the Print command uses the letter P, Import uses the letter I.

As an example, the keyboard shortcut for the Save command is Ctrl+S.

To use the keyboard shortcut for the Save command:

1. Press and hold down the Ctrl key.

2. Press and release the S key.

3. Release the Ctrl key.

Tip:

- Many keyboard shortcuts are listed next to their corresponding commands on the menus.

The Panning Tool; Keyboard Shortcuts

The Zoom Tool; Zoom In

THE ZOOM TOOL

The Zoom Tool is used for magnifying or reducing the view of a drawing. You can zoom in to see detail or zoom out to view an entire drawing. The Property Bar works in concert with the Zoom Tool (**Figure 14**). When the Zoom Tool is selected the Property Bar displays zoom-specific buttons. You can use it to toggle between the Zoom and Panning Tools.

You can also use the Zoom Box on the Standard Toolbar to move to preset and specific magnifications.

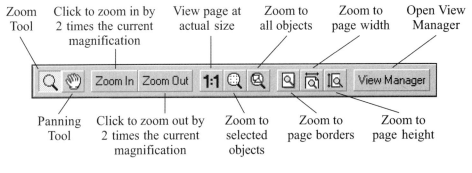

Figure 14. *The Property Bar shows zoom-related buttons when the Zoom Tool is selected.*

To zoom in using the Zoom Tool:

1. Select the Zoom Tool from the Toolbox (**Figure 15**).

2. Position the mouse over the area you want to zoom in on.

3. Click the left mouse button. The view will zoom in 2 times the magnification.

Tip:

■ Zooming has no effect on the drawing, only your view of it.

Figure 15. *Click the Zoom Tool in the Toolbox to select it. The mouse pointer will change to a magnifying glass with a plus on the lens.*

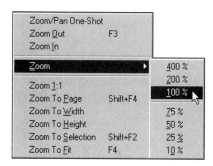

Figure 16. *Select Zoom Out from the pop-up menu or choose a specific magnification from the Zoom fly-out.*

Zoom Box

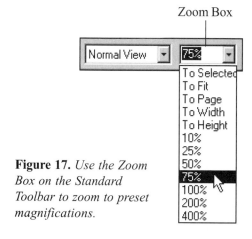

Figure 17. *Use the Zoom Box on the Standard Toolbar to zoom to preset magnifications.*

Figure 18. *Type a number in the Zoom Box then press Enter on the keyboard to zoom to a specific magnification.*

To zoom out using the Zoom Tool:

1. Select the Zoom Tool from the Toolbox (**Figure 15**).

2. Position the mouse over the area you want to zoom out on.

3. Click the right mouse button. A pop-up menu will appear (**Figure 16**).

4. Select Zoom Out or choose a percentage from the Zoom fly-out. The view will zoom out the magnification you selected.

Tip:

■ To zoom out to half the magnification, press F3 on the keyboard.

To zoom using the Standard Toolbar:

1. On the Standard Toolbar near the top of the screen, click the arrow on the Zoom Box to see all the preset magnifications (**Figure 17**).

2. Select a magnification. The view will zoom to that magnification.

Tip:

■ To zoom to a specific magnification, type a number in the drop-down list box (**Figure 18**), then press Enter on the keyboard.

Zoom Out; The Zoom Box

VIEWING A DOCUMENT

The View menu gives you commands for changing the *view quality*. View quality is the way a drawing is displayed in the drawing window. The five view qualities range from displaying only simple outlines to all outlines, complex fills, and bitmap images. They are as follows:

- Simple wireframe—this view hides fills, extrusions, contours, and intermediate blend objects. It shows only simple outlines and monochromatic bitmaps.

- Wireframe—this view hides fills and displays monochromatic bitmaps, extrusions, contours, and intermediate blend objects.

- Draft—this view quality shows some fills and only low-resolution bitmaps.

- Normal—this is the default view. This view quality shows all fills, objects, and high-resolution bitmaps.

- Enhanced—this view uses *oversampling* to enhance the view quality.

In addition, you can view a drawing in Full-Screen Preview mode.

To change the view quality:

1. Open the View menu by clicking the menu title (**Figure 19**).

2. Select the view quality you want to use or Full-Screen Preview from the menu items.

or

Use the View Quality drop-down list on the Standard Toolbar to select a new view quality (**Figure 20**).

Tip:

- To quickly move to Full-Screen Preview mode, press F9 on the keyboard.

Figure 19. *Select the view quality that you want to use from the View menu.*

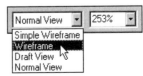

Figure 20. *You can also select view quality from the drop-down list on the Standard Toolbar.*

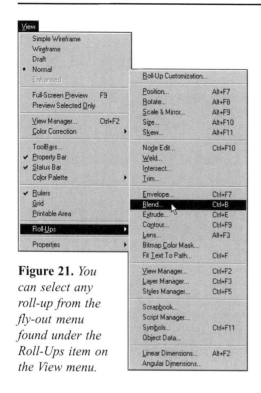

Figure 21. *You can select any roll-up from the fly-out menu found under the Roll-Ups item on the View menu.*

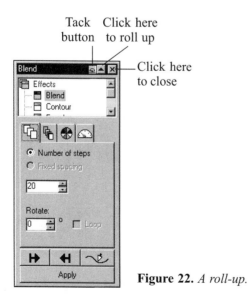

Tack button

Click here to roll up

Click here to close

Figure 22. *A roll-up.*

DESKTOP POWER TOOLS: ROLL-UPS

CorelDraw comes with special floating dialog boxes called *roll-ups*. Unlike most dialog boxes, roll-ups stay on the screen after changes are applied, letting you continue to make changes without having to open the roll-up again. When not using a roll-up, you can minimize it—roll it up—leaving only the title bar visible.

To view a roll-up:

Select a menu command that uses a roll-up such as the Blend or Envelope command on the Effects menu.

or

1. Choose Roll-Ups from the View menu. A gigantic fly-out, containing all the roll-up names appears (**Figure 21**).

2. Select a name from the fly-out list. The roll-up will open (**Figure 22**).

Tip:

■ You can set whether a roll-up will remain open after you click Apply. To keep a roll-up open, "tack" it down by clicking the Tack button.

Power Tools on the Desktop: Roll-Ups

GETTING HELP

CorelDraw 7 comes with a comprehensive help system that has been developed with users' requests in mind. There are seven parts in the help system:

- The User's Guide—this is the paper manual that ships with CorelDraw. You can read it at your leisure, even away from your computer.

- Online Help—built in the standard Windows 95 style, Online Help has three tab pages, set up like a book with Contents, Index, and Find (**Figure 23**).

- Technical Support—if you are having any problems getting CorelDraw to work, check here.

- Hints—this helper displays information about the task that you are performing. When you click a tool or object, the Online Hints window changes to show you information pertaining to the selected item (**Figure 24**).

- Corel Tutor—the Tutor gives you step-by-step instruction on how to complete specific tasks (**Figure 25**). You can even get the Tutor to demonstrate how to do something.

- What's This?—this helper gives you an on-demand description of the tools you are using (**Figure 26**).

- ToolTips—these are the balloons that appear when the mouse passes over a button or drop-down list on a toolbar (**Figure 27**).

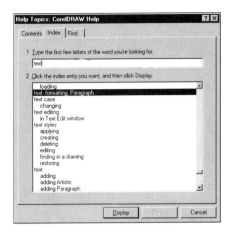

Figure 23. *Online Help.*

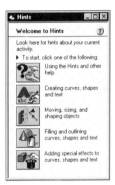

Figure 24. *Hints.*

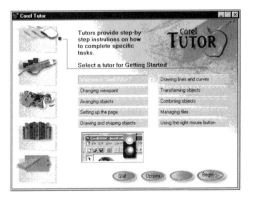

Figure 25. *Corel Tutor.*

Determines the number of actions or operations that can be reversed using the Undo command in the Edit menu. As the setting increases, so does the amount of memory CorelDRAW requires to operate.

Figure 26. *What's This? help.*

Figure 27. *A ToolTip.*

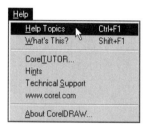

Figure 28. *Select any type of help from the Help menu.*

What's This?
Button

Figure 29.
A What's This? button.

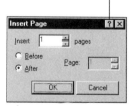

Figure 30.
You can select What's This? from virtually any pop-up menu.

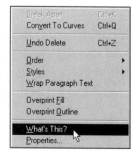

To open Online Help, Technical Support, Hints, or Corel Tutor:

1. Click the Help menu title on the Menu Bar (**Figure 28**).

2. Select the type of help you want.

To use What's This? help:

1. Click the button with the question mark in it, found at the top right of any dialog box (**Figure 29**).

2. Move the mouse pointer over the object you want to know about and click. A help window will appear (**Figure 26**).

or

Right mouse click on an item you are curious about, then select What's This? from the pop-up menu (**Figure 30**).

To see ToolTips:

Slowly move the mouse pointer over any button. A balloon help window will appear, telling you what the button does.

How to Open Help

Object

Everything you create in CorelDraw is an object.

Path

The outside perimeter of an object. A path can be either opened or closed. Paths pass through nodes.

Properties

The attributes of objects, such as fill color, size, and shape.

Objects

Closed path   Open path

Handles

A set of eight black squares that appear in a rectangular formation around a selected object.

Nodes

The clear squares that paths pass through. They can be used to shape paths with the Shape Tool.

Handles

Control Points

The handle that shapes a line segment. Control points are attached to nodes with levers.

Line Segment

The portion of path between two nodes.

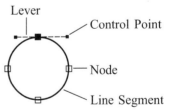

Lever · Control Point · Node · Line Segment

Select

Click with the Pick Tool to select objects and the Shape Tool to select nodes.

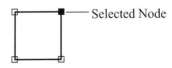

Selected Node

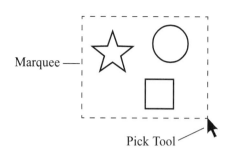

Marquee

Pick Tool

Multiple Select

Press the Shift key while clicking to select several objects or nodes at once.

Marquee Select

Using the Pick or Shape Tools, press the left mouse button and drag to create a dashed rectangle that encloses objects or nodes.

Outline

Uniform Fill

Fountain Fills

Linear — Radial

Conical — Square

Outline

The line representing the path that can be colored or invisible.

Fill

A uniform color, pattern, texture, or fountain fill, added to the inside of an object.

Fountain Fill

A gradual blend from one color to another or a cascade of different colors.

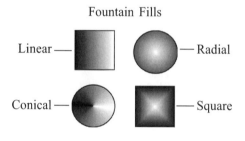

Stacking Order

Guidelines

Non-printing lines that can be used to align objects.

Layer

A transparent plane on which objects are placed when drawing.

Stacking Order

The sequence in which objects are drawn in the drawing window. The first object drawn appears at the bottom of the stack, while the last object drawn is on top.

Group

A set of objects that are combined so they can be moved or modified as a single object.

Nested Group

A grouping of two or more groups that behave as a single object.

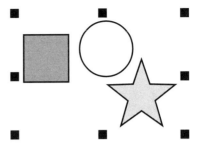

Grouped objects, selected

HARDWARE CONSIDERATIONS

Corel Corporation recommends the following as the minimum system requirements for running CorelDraw 7:

- 60 MHz Pentium with 16 MB RAM and a VGA graphics card.

However, for best performance they recommend:

- 120 MHz Pentium with 32 MB RAM and an SVGA graphics card.

This book was created using a 100 MHz Pentium with 32 MB RAM and an SVGA graphics card with 4 MB RAM. When testing CorelDraw 7, this hardware was fine for creating complex vector graphics, though it was pushed to the limit when working with bitmaps and bitmap filters.

SUMMARY

In this chapter you learned:

- What CorelDraw 7 is
- How CorelDraw works
- About toolbars
- What's in the Toolbox
- About roll-ups

You also learned how to:

- Use a menu
- Use keyboard shortcuts
- Zoom in and out
- View a drawing
- Get help

Startup 2

This chapter starts out by showing you how to launch CorelDraw 7. Next, you'll add a short-cut for CorelDraw 7 to your Windows 95/NT desktop. From there you will create a new document, open an existing one, and save a document. Then you will discover how to import and export graphics, close a document, and exit CorelDraw 7. Finally, you will learn how to restore a damaged CorelDraw file using a backup file.

To launch CorelDraw 7:

1. On the Windows 95/NT desktop, click the Start button on the Status Bar, move up to the Programs item, and select it.

2. On the Programs fly-out select the CorelDraw 7 program folder. (This is the default location where the CorelDraw 7 installation places the program group.)

3. On the fly-out, click CorelDraw 7 (**Figure 1**).

Figure 1. *Launching CorelDraw 7.*

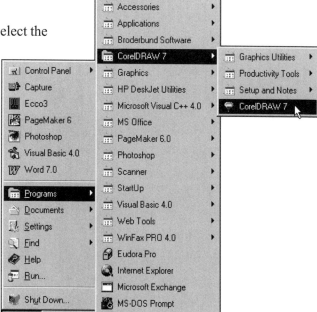

To put a shortcut to CorelDraw 7 on the Windows 95/NT desktop:

1. *Right* mouse click on the Start button and select Explore from the pop-up menu (**Figure 2**). This will open the Windows Explorer with the Start Menu folder near the bottom of the left pane.

2. Click on the plus sign next to the Programs folder which resides under the Start Menu folder (**Figure 3**). This will expand the Programs folder.

3. Under the expanded Programs folder, select the CorelDraw 7 folder (**Figure 4**). The right pane of Explorer will display several folders and a CorelDraw 7 shortcut.

4. Move to the right pane of Explorer and, using the right mouse button, click and drag the CorelDraw 7 shortcut from the Explorer window onto the Windows 95/NT desktop.

5. Release the mouse button. A pop-up menu will appear on the desktop.

6. Click Create Shortcut(s) Here (**Figure 5**). The CorelDraw 7 shortcut will appear on the desktop.

Figure 2. *Right mouse click on the Start button and select Explore.*

Figure 3. *Click on the plus sign next to Programs under the Start Menu folder.*

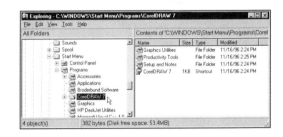

Figure 4. *Under the Programs folder, select CorelDraw 7.*

Figure 5. *Click Create Shortcut(s) Here on the pop-up menu.*

Make a CorelDraw 7 Shortcut

Figure 6. *The CorelDraw 7 Welcome Screen.*

When you launch CorelDraw 7 for the very first time, you will see the Welcome Screen (**Figure 6**). This window displays five options that you can select:

- Start a new graphic
- Open the last file you worked on
- Open an existing CorelDraw file
- Use a template as the basis for a new document
- Start CorelTutor
- Find out what's new

To choose any one of these options, click the button next to the desired item.

If you do not want to see the Welcome Screen every time you launch the program, be sure to remove the check from the check box at the bottom of the screen. If you do uncheck the box, CorelDraw will automatically open a new document for you every time you launch the program (this is the same as the "Start a New CorelDraw Graphic" option on the Welcome Screen).

To start a new document:

If you decide to remove the Welcome Screen as described above, CorelDraw will automatically start a new document for you every time you launch the program.

If you are already working in CorelDraw and want to start a new document, select New from the File menu (**Figure 7**) or press Ctrl+N on the keyboard.

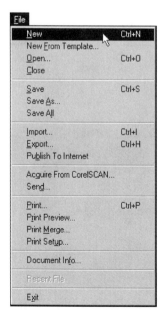

Figure 7. *To start a new document, select New on the File menu.*

ocuments can be based on a CorelDraw *template*. Templates are special, predesigned files that help you quickly create professional-looking documents such as greeting cards, business cards, and brochures.

To start a new document using a template:

1. Select New From Template from the File menu (**Figure 8**). The Template Wizard will open (**Figure 9**).

2. Select what type of template you would like to use. CorelDraw 7 ships with over 450 templates, many of which are designed for PaperDirect pre-printed papers.

3. When you have selected the template type you want to use, click Next to move to the next Wizard panel (**Figure 10**).

4. On the second panel, select the type of document you would like to create—brochure, label, postcard, etc.

Figure 8. *Select New From Template from the File menu.*

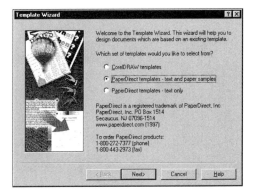

Figure 9. *Select the type of template you want to use.*

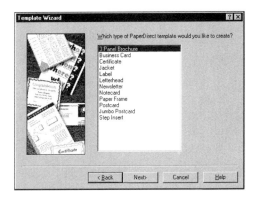

Figure 10. *Select the type of document you want to create.*

New Template Document

Preview Pane

Figure 11. *Select the template design that fits your project best.*

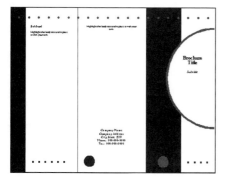

Figure 12. *When the Wizard is finished, a new document is created using the template you selected as a guide.*

Figure 13. *Select Open from the File menu.*

5. Click Next to move to the third panel (**Figure 11**).

6. Select a design from the template list, using the preview pane to see what it looks like.

7. Put a check mark in the Open with contents check box to have the document created with the template design.

8. Click Finish. The Wizard will close and a new document will be created from the template, ready for your modifications (**Figure 12**).

To open an existing document:

1. Select Open from the File menu (**Figure 13**) or press Ctrl+O on your keyboard. The Open Drawing dialog box will appear (**Figure 14**).

2. Move to the folder where the document is stored, then choose the CorelDraw file you want to access and click Open.

Figure 14. *Highlight the file you want to open, then press the Open button.*

Open a Document

To save your work:

1. Select Save from the File menu (**Figure 15**) or press Ctrl+S on the keyboard. The Save Drawing dialog box will appear (**Figure 16**).

2. Move to the folder where you want to save the drawing, then type a name in the File name text box.

3. Click the Save button.

To save a copy of a file:

1. Open the file you want to copy.

2. Select Save As from the File menu (**Figure 17**). The Save Drawing dialog box will open (**Figure 16**).

3. Move to the folder where you want to save the copy and modify the file name that is there in the File name text box or type in a new name.

4. Click the Save button.

Figure 15. *Select Save from the File menu.*

Figure 16. *Use the Save Drawing dialog box to name your file and save your work.*

Figure 17. *To save a copy of a drawing, use Save As on the File menu.*

THERE'S ALWAYS A WAY OUT!

If you find yourself in a window that you did not mean to use, don't panic! Remember that you can always press the Cancel button.

Save Your Work; Save a Copy of a File

Figure 18. *To import a graphic, select Import from the File menu.*

You can import many types of files—CorelDraw clipart, text, graphics CAD drawings, etc—into your projects. (For an easy way to import CorelDraw graphics using the Scrapbook roll-up, see Chapter 16.)

To import a file:

1. Select Import from the File menu (**Figure 18**) or press Ctrl+I on the keyboard. The Import dialog box will open.

2. Move to the folder where the file is stored and highlight the file you want to import. To see a preview of the image, make sure a check appears in the box next to Preview on the right side of the window (**Figure 19**).

3. To see more information about the file you are about to import, press the Options button at the lower right of the window (**Figure 19**). The bottom of the window will expand to give you information about the filter being used, the file's format and size, etc. (**Figure 20**).

4. Click the Import button. The file will appear, selected, in your document.

Figure 19. *The Import dialog box.*

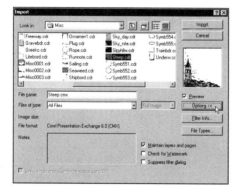

Figure 20. *Press the Options button to learn more about the graphic you are going to import.*

Every image you see in *CorelDraw 7 for Windows 95/NT: Visual QuickStart Guide*, has either been designed by me or is a piece of clipart from the CorelDraw CD-ROM disks. If you see a clipart image you want to use for your own drawing, look in Appendix A to find the exact location of the image.

Import a File

To export a drawing:

1. Select the drawing that you want to export.

2. Open the Export dialog box by selecting Export from the File menu (**Figure 21**) or press Ctrl+H on the keyboard.

3. Move to the folder where you would like to store the graphic, then type a name in the File name text box (**Figure 22**).

4. Select the file type you want to save the graphic as, by clicking the down arrow next to the Save as type drop-down list, and selecting a file type (**Figure 23**).

5. If the graphic that you are exporting is part of a larger graphic (in other words, you selected a portion of a drawing before you opened the Export window), make sure that the Selected only check box in the lower right corner is checked (**Figure 24**).

6. Click the Export button. Depending upon the file type you selected, a Bitmap Export dialog box will open, displaying the possible settings for that file type (**Figure 25**). In this dialog box you can set:

   - The number of colors with which the graphic will be exported

   - The image size

   - The image resolution in *dots per inch* (dpi)

Figure 21. *To export a drawing, select Export from the File menu.*

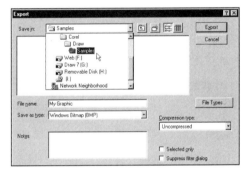

Figure 22. *Use the Export dialog box to select the location where you want to put the file and the type of file that you want to export.*

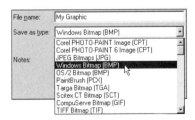

Figure 23. *Press the down arrow next to the Save as type list box to select a file format.*

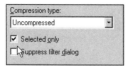

Figure 24. *If you are exporting a portion of a drawing, make sure the Selected only box in the Export window is checked.*

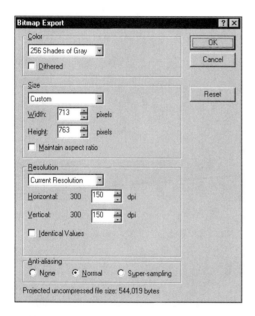

Figure 25. *The Bitmap Export dialog box lets you set the number of colors, size, and resolution of the drawing you are exporting.*

Remember that the higher any of these settings are—more colors, a larger image size, higher image resolution—the larger the file. Using larger sized files means that display time on your computer will increase and printing the files will take much longer (sometimes hours!).

7. When you are happy with the settings, press OK.

Tips:

■ Before you export a graphic that is made up of more than one object, be sure you *group* the objects together, otherwise your graphic will not export correctly. (Grouping objects together is discussed on page 182.)

■ Always try to get away with using the least amount of colors and the lowest resolution you can. You might have to export the image a few times until you get the desired effect, but smaller images mean time saved for you when you load or print the graphic.

■ If you change the resolution settings, make sure the Identical Values box is checked. Many printers cannot handle different horizontal and vertical resolutions. Also, the result that different horizontal and vertical resolutions might have could be pretty ugly.

Export a Drawing

File Extensions

File extensions are the three letters that come after the period in a file name. For instance, the file MyFile.Cdr has a file extension of .Cdr. These file extensions tell the computer (and the human!) what kind of file it is and how to interpret it.

CorelDraw uses several file extensions:

- .Cdr–this is the native CorelDraw file extension that will automatically be attached to your documents when you save them.
- .Cdt–CorelDraw Template
- .Cmx–Corel Presentation Exchange

Other file extensions that you may see in your journey as a CorelDraw graphics artist:

- .Cpt–Corel PhotoPaint
- .Bmp–Windows bitmap
- .Eps–Encapsulated PostScript file
- .Tif–Tag Image File Format (Tiff) bitmap

If you surf the World Wide Web, you will probably see these formats used:

- .Gif–CompuServe bitmap
- .Jpg–Joint Photographic Experts Group (Jpeg) bitmap

For more information about the .Gif and .Jpg file formats, take a look at Chapter 17, *Creating Graphics for the Web*.

How to View File Extensions in Windows 95/NT

To see all file extensions, open any Windows 95/NT window—for instance, double click on My Computer to open that window—and select Options from the View menu. In the Options dialog box, click the View tab to bring that tab page to the front. For Windows 95, make sure that the check box next to "Hide MS-DOS file extensions for file types that are registered" is unchecked. For Windows NT, make sure that the check box next to "Hide file extensions for known file types" is unchecked.

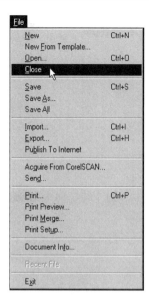

Figure 26. *To close a document select Close from the File menu.*

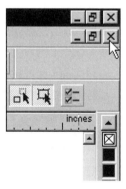

Figure 27. *To close a document, press the Close button at the upper right-hand corner of the document window.*

To close a document:

Select Close from the File menu (**Figure 26**).

or

Press Ctrl+F4 on the keyboard.

or

Click on the Close button (**Figure 27**) at the upper right-hand corner of the document window.

Tip:

■ If the document you are closing has not been recently saved, CorelDraw will automatically ask whether you want to save it.

HOW MANY DOCUMENTS CAN I HAVE OPEN AT ONCE?

The number of CorelDraw documents you can have open at one time is only limited by the amount of RAM you have in your computer.

Close a Document

31

Somctimes files become corrupted. If you try to open a CorelDraw file and it does not function properly, don't panic! CorelDraw is set to automatically make backups of all your drawings. You can use these backup files to restore a corrupted file.

Figure 28. *Select Options from the Tools menu.*

To set backup options:

1. Select Options from the Tools menu (**Figure 28**) or press Ctrl+J on the keyboard. The Options dialog box will open (**Figure 29**).

2. Click on the Advanced tab to bring that tab page to the front (**Figure 30**).

3. Make sure there is a check mark in the Auto-backup check box. By default, a backup will be made every 10 minutes. You can change this number to suit your needs (and personality).

4. Set the place where the backup file will be stored using the options buttons. By default the backup is placed in the same folder as the file that it backs up. You can change this to a specific folder, if you desire.

Tip:

- Don't set the auto-backup time to less than 5 minutes. If you are working on a large file, saving it can slow your computer down and interrupt your work.

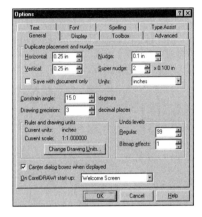

Figure 29. *The Options dialog box with the General tab page in front.*

Figure 30. *Use the Auto-Backup area on the Advanced tab page, to change auto-backup settings.*

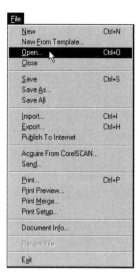

Figure 31. *To restore a file using a backup, select Open from the File menu.*

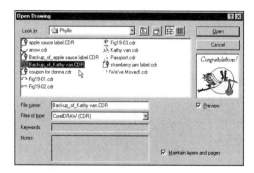

Figure 32. *The backup file will have "Backup_of_" added before the original file name. Select the backup file name that matches the original.*

To restore a corrupted file:

1. Select Open from the File menu (**Figure 31**). The Open Drawing dialog box will display (**Figure 32**).

2. Move to the folder where the backup is stored. By default, this is the same folder where the original file lives.

3. Auto-backup files have "Backup_of_" added before the original file name. Select the backup file name that matches the corrupted original file name. For example, if the original corrupted file is named Train.Cdr, select Backup_of_Train.Cdr).

4. Click Open. The backup will open.

5. Save the backup using Save As on the File menu to rename the file without the "Backup_of_" prefix.

Tip:

■ Remember that a backup file is generated only periodically, so the backup may not be "up to the minute." It may have been made five or eight minutes before the original file was corrupted. But, an older backup file is better than no file at all!

Restore a Corrupted File

To exit CorelDraw:

Select Exit from the File Menu
(**Figure 33**)

or

Press Alt+F4 on the keyboard

or

Click the Close button in the extreme
upper right-hand corner of the screen
(**Figure 34**).

Tip:

■ When you exit CorelDraw, all
open files will close. If changes
have been made to an open file
since it was last saved, CorelDraw
will automatically ask whether
you want to save it.

Figure 33. *To exit CorelDraw 7, select Exit from the File menu.*

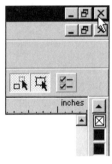

Figure 34. *Another way to exit CorelDraw is to click the Close button in the extreme upper-right corner of the screen.*

SUMMARY

In this chapter you learned how to:

■ Launch CorelDraw   ■ Import and export a graphic

■ Start a new document   ■ Close a document

■ Open an existing document   ■ Restore a file using backup

■ Save your work   ■ Exit CorelDraw

Exit CorelDraw 7

Rectangles and Ellipses

Paths, Objects, and Properties

This chapter will get you started on the road to creating fantastic graphics with CorelDraw 7. The simple shapes you create here are the basis for every drawing, no matter how complex. (Check out the train on this page. It's mostly simple rectangles and circles, but the complete drawing is rather complex—more than 150 objects!)

In this chapter you will draw rectangles and squares, and round their corners. Next, you will create ellipses and circles, then manipulate one of their *properties*, making them into pie shapes and arcs. Finally, you will learn how to set the default drawing settings for the Ellipse Tool.

Everything you create using the tools in CorelDraw 7, whether it's a line, a triangle, or a circle, has a *path*. Paths can be either *open* or *closed*. The beginning and end of an open path do not connect. For instance, a line is an open path. A closed path has no distinct beginning or end, just as a circle or rectangle has no beginning or end. In other words, a closed path is a *shape*.

In CorelDraw, a line or shape is also known as an *object*. The outside perimeter of an object is a path. In addition, every object has *properties* that can be set. These properties include such items as the object's size, shape, and position.

To draw a rectangle:

1. Choose the Rectangle Tool (**Figure 1**). Your mouse pointer will change to a cross-hair with a little rectangle connected to it.

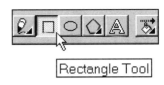

Figure 1. *The Rectangle Tool.*

2. Press the left mouse button down and drag it diagonally (**Figure 2**). As you drag, the rectangle will appear. When you release the mouse, the rectangle will be selected, showing four *nodes*, one at each corner (**Figure 3**). (Nodes are discussed in Chapter 6, *Nodes and Paths*.)

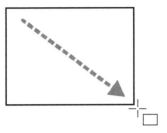

Figure 2. *Drag the mouse diagonally to draw the rectangle.*

Tips:

- To draw a perfect square, hold down the Ctrl key while you drag the mouse. Make sure you release the mouse button first, otherwise the object will spring back to a non-symmetrical shape.

- Remember that you can change the outline color or fill of any closed path object that you create (fills and outlines are discussed in Chapter 10, *Color and Fills*).

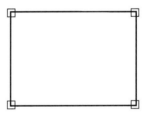

Figure 3. *When you release the mouse button, the rectangle will be selected, showing four nodes.*

Draw a Rectangle

HOW TO DRAW AN OBJECT FROM THE CENTER

Hold down the Shift key while dragging the mouse to draw a rectangle or ellipse from the center. When your object is the desired size, release the mouse button first, otherwise, the object will spring closer to the mouse pointer and be created from its edge.

Figure 4. *Select the Pick Tool from the Toolbox.*

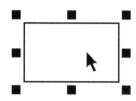

Figure 5. *Click on the rectangle with the Pick Tool to select it.*

Figure 6. *Move the Rectangle Corner Roundness slider or type a setting in the text box to the right of it on the Property Bar.*

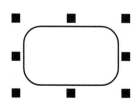

Figure 7. *The rounded rectangle.*

To round the corners of a rectangle:

1. Select the Pick Tool from the Toolbox (**Figure 4**).

2. Click on the rectangle to select it. Eight black squares, *handles*, will appear around the rectangle (**Figure 5**).

3. On the Property Bar near the top of the screen, enter a number in the Rectangle Corner Roundness text box or drag the slider bar to the right (**Figure 6**). The corners of the rectangle will become rounded (**Figure 7**).

Tips:

■ The larger the number or further to the right the slider bar is, the rounder the corners will be.

■ If the Property Bar is not displayed, you can open it by choosing Property Bar from the View menu (**Figure 8**).

Figure 8. *To display the Property Bar, choose Property Bar from the View menu.*

Round the Corners of a Rectangle

To create an ellipse:

1. Select the Ellipse Tool (**Figure 9**). Your mouse pointer will change to a cross-hair with an attached ellipse.

2. Press the left mouse button down and drag it diagonally (**Figure 10**). As you drag, the ellipse will appear. When you release the mouse, the ellipse will be selected, displaying one node at the top (**Figure 11**).

Tip:

■ To draw a perfect circle, press down the Ctrl key while you drag the mouse. Release the mouse button first when you are finished dragging or the circle will spring to an elliptical shape.

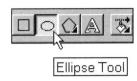

Figure 9. *The Ellipse Tool.*

Figure 10. *Drag the mouse diagonally to create the ellipse.*

Figure 11. *When you release the mouse button, the ellipse will be selected, displaying one node at the top.*

DRAWING SYMMETRICAL OBJECTS FROM THE CENTER

To create a perfectly symmetrical object such as a circle or square from the center, hold down both the Ctrl and Shift keys while dragging the mouse.

Figure 12. *Click on the ellipse with the Pick Tool to select it.*

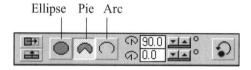

Figure 13. *Click the Pie or Arc buttons on the Property Bar to change the ellipse to one of those shapes.*

Figure 14. *When you click the Pie button, the ellipse changes to a pie shape.*

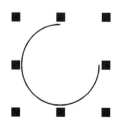

Figure 15. *When you click the Arc button on the Property Bar, the ellipse changes to an arc.*

To change an ellipse into a pie shape or arc:

1. Select the Pick Tool from the Toolbox (**Figure 4**).

2. Click on the ellipse to select it (**Figure 12**). Eight black handles will appear around the ellipse.

3. To change the ellipse to a pie shape, click the Pie button on the Property Bar (**Figure 13**). The ellipse will change to a pie shape (**Figure 14**).

   or

   To change the ellipse to an arc, click the Arc button on the Property Bar. The ellipse will change to an arc (**Figure 15**).

Tip:

- You can use the Property Bar to set the starting and ending angles for pie shapes and arcs, as well as their direction of rotation, clockwise or counterclockwise (**Figure 16**).

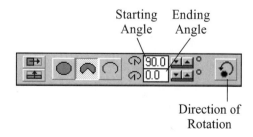

Figure 16. *You can use the Property Bar to change the starting and ending angles and rotation direction of pie shapes and arcs.*

Change an Ellipse to a Pie Shape or Arc

Y ou can change the default properties of the Ellipse Tool to make it always draw pie shapes or arcs.

Figure 17. *When you right mouse click on the Ellipse Tool a pop-up menu appears. Select Properties.*

To change the Ellipse Tool's defaults:

1. Right mouse click on the Ellipse Tool in the Toolbar. A pop-up menu will appear (**Figure 17**).

2. Select Properties from the pop-up menu. The Options dialog box will appear with the Toolbox tab page in front and the Ellipse Tool selected (**Figure 18**).

3. In the Ellipse tool defaults area, select the type of shape you would like to draw, Pie or Arc, using the option buttons. Then set the starting and ending angles and rotation direction.

4. Click OK. Every time you use the Ellipse Tool from now on, the tool will draw the shape you specified (**Figure 19**).

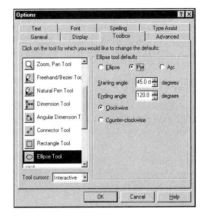

Figure 18. *Use the Ellipse tool defaults area of the Toolbox tab page to set new Ellipse tool defaults.*

Tip:

- You can always change the tool back to its original default by using the steps outlined above and selecting Ellipse.

Figure 19.
After changing the defaults, the Ellipse Tool draws what you selected.

Change Ellipse Tool Defaults

SUMMARY

In this chapter you learned how to:

- Draw rectangles
- Round a rectangle's corners
- Draw ellipses

- Make an ellipse into a pie shape or an arc
- Set the Ellipse Tool's defaults

Select, Move, and Size

n Chapter 3 you learned how to draw simple shapes such as squares and circles. Now it's time to learn how to select, move, copy, and resize them. The tool you will use to do all this is one you've already used, the *Pick Tool* (**Figure 1**).

Figure 1. *The Pick Tool.*

The Pick Tool is used to select objects and also manipulate an object's *handles*. Handles are the large black squares that appear in a rectangular formation around an object when it is selected by the Pick Tool (**Figure 2**). They are used to change the overall shape of an object.

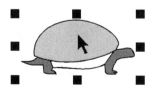

Figure 2. *Handles appear around an object when it is selected with the Pick Tool. Handles are used to horizontally and vertically size an object.*

To select an object:

1. Select the Pick Tool from the Toolbox.

2. Click on the object. Eight black handles will appear around the object (**Figure 3**).

To select multiple objects by clicking:

1. Select the Pick Tool from the Toolbox.

2. Hold down the Shift key while clicking on the objects you want to select. As you select objects, the handles' rectangular formation will expand to include the objects (**Figure 4**).

To select multiple objects by dragging (marquee select):

1. Make sure the Pick Tool is selected, then place the pointer arrow to the left of the objects you want to select.

2. Press the left mouse button down and drag it to select the objects. As you drag, a dashed blue rectangle, or *marquee*, will appear, indicating the selected area (**Figure 5**).

3. Release the mouse button when the marquee encompasses the objects you want to select. The items will be selected as a group with the eight handles appearing in a rectangular formation around the objects (**Figure 6**).

Figure 3. *Handles appear around an object when it is selected.*

Figure 4. *The handles' rectangular formation expands to include each object as it is selected. In this case, the bunny and flowers are selected, whereas the t-rex and crown are not.*

Figure 5. *As you drag the mouse to select multiple objects, a dashed rectangle, or marquee, appears around the selected area.*

Figure 6. *When the mouse is released, handles appear around the selected objects.*

Figure 7. *To select all objects on a page, choose Select All from the Edit menu.*

To select all objects on a page:

Choose Select All on the Edit Menu (**Figure 7**) or double-click on the Pick Tool in the Toolbox.

To deselect an object:

1. Select the Pick Tool.

2. Click outside the selected object.

or

Press the Esc key on the keyboard.

Tip:

- To deselect one object within a multiple selection, hold down the Shift key and click on that object.

To move an object:

1. Position the Pick Tool over the object.

2. Press the left mouse button and drag the object to its new location. As you drag, a marquee and wireframe representation of the object will follow along with your pointer until you release the mouse button (**Figure 8**).

Figure 8. *As you move an object, a marquee and wireframe representation of the object appear on the screen. The object itself remains stationary until you release the mouse.*

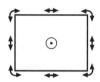

Figure 9. *Double-headed arrows appear around an object when you double-click on it or click once with the object already selected.*

What Are Those Funny Double-headed Arrows Around My Object?

If you click on a selected object—one whose handles are already visible—the handles will change to double-headed arrows (**Figure 9**). These arrows are used to skew and rotate an object and will be discussed in Chapter 12 and Chapter 14. To get the big black handles back again, click on the object.

here are two ways to copy an object: by copying the object to the Windows Clipboard and then pasting it into the document, or by duplicating the object. The end result of these two procedures is the same, but the amount of computing power they use is very different.

Figure 10. *Choose Copy from the Edit Menu.*

To copy an object using the Windows Clipboard:

1. Use the Pick Tool to select the object you want to copy.

2. Choose Copy from the Edit menu (**Figure 10**) or press Ctrl+C on the keyboard to copy the object to the Windows Clipboard.

3. Choose Paste from the Edit menu (**Figure 11**) or press Ctrl+V on the keyboard. A copy of the object will appear, selected, directly on top of the original. To move the copy, place the the Pick Tool over the copy (not on the object's black handles), press the left mouse button, and drag the object to another position (**Figure 12**).

Figure 11. *Choose Paste from the Edit menu.*

Figure 12. *As you drag the copy to a new position, a dashed rectangle appears around the object.*

COPYING USING THE CLIPBOARD VS. DUPLICATING

If you copy an object to the Clipboard, you can then paste it to other pages in your CorelDraw document. It will also be available to other Windows 95 programs. For instance, you could paste a rectangle copied from CorelDraw into Microsoft Word. However, copying and pasting an object, especially a complex one, will put your computer to work for a long time.

CorelDraw's duplicate command bypasses the Clipboard, making it a fast operation. In addition, you can specify exactly where a duplicate will appear in relation to the original (see page 191), whereas a copy will always appear on top of the original.

Copy an Object *(side margin)*

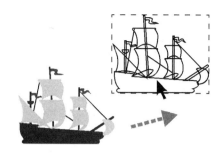

Figure 13. *As you drag with the right button depressed, a wireframe copy of the original appears on the screen.*

Figure 14. *Select Copy Here from the pop-up menu.*

Figure 15. *Choose Duplicate from the Edit menu.*

To copy an object by dragging:

1. Position the Pick Tool's over the object you want to copy.

2. Press the *right* mouse button and drag the mouse. As you drag, a wireframe version of the object will appear on the screen (**Figure 13**).

3. Release the mouse button. A pop-up menu will appear. Click on Copy Here (**Figure 14**).

To duplicate an object:

1. Select the object to be duplicated using the Pick Tool.

2. Choose Duplicate from the Edit menu (**Figure 15**) or press Ctrl+D on the keyboard. The duplicate will appear, selected, to the right and slightly above the original by default (**Figure 16**).

Tip:

■ Another quick way to duplicate an object is to press the ⊞ key on your keypad. This duplicates the object, and places it directly on top of the original.

Figure 16. *The duplicate appears slightly above and to the right of the original.*

Copy by Dragging; Duplicate an Object

Handles appear in a rectangular formation around an object when it is selected with the Pick Tool. These handles have various functions:

■ The handles that appear to the right center and left center of the object affect the object's *horizontal scale*—they will make an object wider or thinner (**Figure 17**).

■ The handles that appear at the top center and bottom center of an object affect the object's *vertical scale* and will make an object taller or shorter (**Figure 18**).

■ The handles that appear at the corners affect the object's *proportional scale*. These handles will let you change the horizontal and vertical size of an object equally (**Figure 19**).

Figure 17. *The handles at the left center and right center of a selected object affect the object's width.*

Figure 18. *The handles at the top center and bottom center of a selected object affect the object's height.*

Figure 19. *The handles at the corners of a selected object affect the object's height and width equally.*

THE PROPERTY BAR CAN BE USED TO EXACTLY SIZE AND POSITION AN OBJECT

To use the Property Bar to size and position an object, select the object with the Pick Tool, then use the text boxes and spin buttons at the left of the bar.

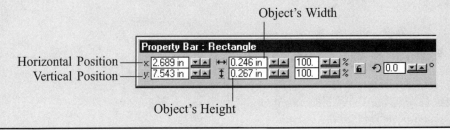

Press Here ■   ■ — Or Press
                          Here

Figure 20. *Drag either the left or right handle to make an object wider or skinnier.*

Figure 21. *As you drag inward, a marquee and wireframe version of the resized object appear on the screen. The original remains stationary until the mouse is released.*

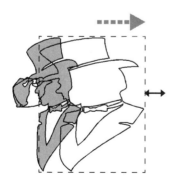

Figure 22. *As you drag outward, a marquee and wireframe version of the resized object appear. The original remains stationary until the mouse is released.*

To change an object's width:

1. Select the object using the Pick Tool.

2. Position the pointer over either the left center or right center handle (**Figure 20**). Press the left mouse button and horizontally drag the handle. As you drag, a blue dash rectangle will appear along with a wireframe representation of the resized object. In addition, the mouse pointer will change to a double-headed horizontal arrow. If you drag the handle toward the object, it will become skinnier (**Figure 21**). If you drag the handle away from the object, it will become fatter (**Figure 22**).

3. Release the mouse button when you are happy with the width.

Tip:

■ You can keep an eye on the object's new width by watching the horizontal ruler bar at the top of the screen.

Change an Object's Width

To change an object's height:

1. Select the object using the Pick Tool.

2. Position the pointer over either the top center or bottom center handle (**Figure 23**). Press the left mouse button and vertically drag the handle. As you drag, a blue dash rectangle will appear along with a wireframe representation of the resized object. Also, the mouse pointer will change to a double-headed vertical arrow. If you drag the handle toward the object, it will become shorter (**Figure 24**). If you drag the handle away from the object, it will become taller (**Figure 25**).

3. Release the mouse button when the object is appropriately short or tall.

Tip:

■ You can keep an eye on the object's new height by watching the vertical ruler bar at the left of the screen.

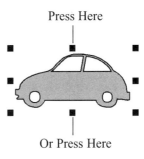

Figure 23. *To change an object's height use either the top center or bottom center handle.*

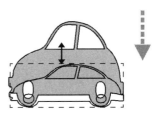

Figure 24. *As you drag the handle toward the object, a marquee and wireframe version of the shorter object appear. The object itself remains stationary until the mouse is released.*

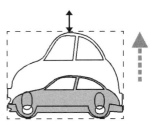

Figure 25. *As you drag the handle away from the object, a marquee and wireframe version of the taller object appear. The object itself stays stationary until you release the mouse button.*

Press Here   Or Here

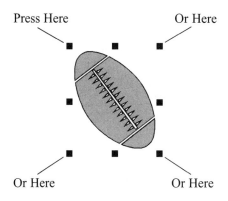

Or Here   Or Here

Figure 26. *The handles at the corners of an object are used to proportionally resize the object's height and width.*

To proportionally change an object's width and height:

1. Select the object with the Pick Tool.

2. Press the left mouse button and diagonally drag any one of the corner handles (**Figure 26**). As you drag a blue dash rectangle and wireframe representation of the resized image will appear. In addition, the mouse pointer will change to a four-headed arrow shaped like an X. If you drag toward the object, it will become smaller (**Figure 27**). If you drag away from the object, it will become larger (**Figure 28**).

3. Release the mouse button when you are happy with the object's new size.

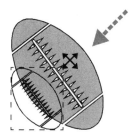

Figure 27. *As you drag a corner handle toward an object, it becomes proportionally smaller.*

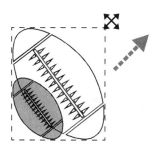

Figure 28. *As you diagonally drag a corner handle away from an object, it becomes proportionally larger.*

MORE ABOUT DRAGGING HANDLES

■ To scale an object from its center, hold down the Shift key while dragging a handle.

■ Press the Ctrl key while dragging a handle to resize the object in 100 percent increments.

Proportionally Scale an Object

To delete an object:

1. Select the object using the Pick Tool.

2. Choose Delete from the Edit menu (**Figure 29**) or press the Delete key on the keyboard.

Tip:

■ If you press the Backspace key instead of the Delete key, nothing will happen.

Figure 29. *To delete an object, select it then choose Delete from the Edit menu.*

THE TAB KEY AND SELECTING

When working with several objects that are close together or on top of each other, it can be difficult to click on the object you want to select.

You can use the keyboard to select the correct object by clicking on an object in your drawing with the Pick Tool, then successively pressing the Tab key until the correct object is selected. As you press the Tab key, watch the Status Bar. It will give you information about which object is currently selected.

SUMMARY

In this chapter you learned how to:

■ Select and move an object

■ Select all objects on a page

■ Marquee select objects

■ Copy and duplicate objects

■ Resize objects horizontally and vertically

■ Proportionally resize an object

■ Delete an object

Delete an Object

Polygons, Stars, and Spirals

CorelDraw makes it easier than ever to create complex objects with just a simple click and drag of the mouse. Using the Polygon and Spiral tools found on the Shape fly-out, shown in **Figure 1**, you can quickly draw polygons, stars, and spirals. The techniques you learn in this chapter will enable you to add dynamic professional-quality effects to your documents and presentations.

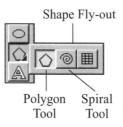

Shape Fly-out

Polygon Tool   Spiral Tool

Figure 1. *The Shape fly-out.*

In this chapter you will learn how to create multi-sided polygons using the Polygon Tool. Then you will discover how to access the Toolbox tab page of the Options dialog box to specify the number of sides a polygon will have. From there, you will use the same Toolbox tab page to create several different types of stars and specify how many points each star has and the depth of each star's interior angles. Finally, you will use the Spiral Tool to create fantastic spirals with just a click and drag of the mouse.

To create a polygon:

1. Choose the Polygon Tool from the CorelDraw Toolbox (**Figure 2**). Your mouse pointer will change to a cross-hair with a little polygon attached to it.

2. Press the left mouse button and drag it diagonally (**Figure 3**). The polygon will appear as you drag the mouse, becoming larger as you pull diagonally. When you release the mouse button, small nodes will appear around the polygon's perimeter and the polygon will be selected.

Tip:

■ Remember that you can change the outline color or fill of any closed path object that you create (see Chapter 3 for a discussion of closed path objects).

Figure 2. *Select the Polygon Tool from the Toolbox.*

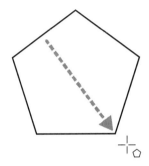

Figure 3. *Drag the mouse diagonally to create the polygon.*

HOW TO DRAW AN OBJECT FROM THE CENTER

Hold down the Shift key while dragging the mouse to draw a polygon from the center. When your object is the desired size, release the mouse button first, otherwise the object will spring closer to your mouse pointer and be created from its edge.

DRAWING PERFECTLY SYMMETRICAL OBJECTS

If you want to create a perfectly symmetrical object, hold down the Ctrl key while dragging the mouse. Be sure to release the mouse button before you let go of the Ctrl key, otherwise your object will spring to a non-symmetrical shape.

Draw a Polygon

Figure 4. *Click with the right mouse button on the Polygon Tool to access Properties from the pop-up menu.*

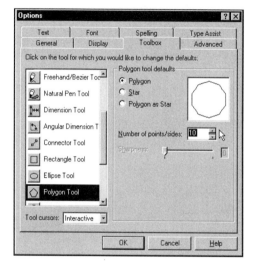

Figure 5. *Use the Options dialog box to set the number of sides a polygon will have.*

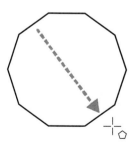

Figure 6. *Drag the mouse diagonally to create a custom polygon.*

To set the number of sides a polygon will have:

1. Double-click on the Polygon Tool in the Toolbox or right mouse click on the Polygon Tool and select Properties from the pop-up menu (**Figure 4**). The Options dialog box will open with the Toolbox tab page in front and Polygon Tool selected (**Figure 5**).

2. Use the spin buttons to the right of the Number of points/sides text box to change the number in the text box or type the desired number in the text box. A preview of the polygon will appear in the window's preview pane. When you are happy with the polygon's shape, click OK.

3. With the Polygon Tool selected, press the left mouse button and drag it diagonally to draw a polygon with the number of sides you just specified (**Figure 6**).

Tip:

■ When you change the Polygon Tool's *Number of points/sides* setting, the new setting will only affect polygons drawn after you changed the setting. Any polygons previously created will remain as they were.

■ You can set a polygon to have as few as 3 sides (a triangle) or as many as 500 sides!

Set the Polygon's Number of Sides

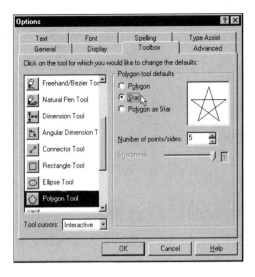

Stars are an extension of the simple polygon shape. The Polygon Tool is used to create stars. You may have already noticed that the Toolbox tab page of the Options dialog box (**Figure 7**) includes the choice of two star types: *Star* and *Polygon as star*.

Figure 7. *Use the Toolbox tab in the Options dialog box to select Star as the default Polygon Tool shape.*

To draw a star:

1. Double-click on the Polygon Tool found in the Toolbox or right mouse click on the Polygon Tool and select Properties from the pop-up menu. The Options dialog box will open with the Toolbox tab to the front and Polygon Tool selected.

2. Select the Star option button (**Figure 7**).

3. Set the number of points you want the star to have using the text box and spin buttons. If the number of points is 7 or more, the Sharpness slider bar and text box will become enabled. A higher sharpness setting will make each of the star's angles sharper (**Figures 8a–b**).

4. Click OK.

5. Using the Polygon Tool, hold down the left mouse button and drag it diagonally (**Figure 9**). The star will appear as you drag the mouse, becoming larger as you pull diagonally. When you release the mouse button the star will be selected.

Figure 8a. *This is a 10-sided star with a Sharpness setting of 1.*

Figure 8b. *This is also a 10-sided star with a Sharpness setting of 3.*

Figure 9. *Drag the mouse diagonally to create the star.*

Draw a Star

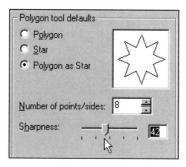

Figure 10. *The Polygon as Star setting creates stars with only an outline. You can use the Sharpness slider bar to change the star's angles.*

Figure 11. *Drag the Polygon Tool diagonally to create a polygon as star.*

Figures 12a–c.

To create a polygon as star:

1. Double-click on the Polygon Tool found in the Toolbox or right mouse click on the Polygon Tool and select Properties from the pop-up menu. The Options dialog box will open with the Toolbox tab to the front and Polygon Tool selected (**Figure 7**).

2. Select the Polygon as Star option button. The star that appears in the preview pane is different from the star in the preceding section in that its lines don't cross (**Figure 10**). Only a star outline is visible.

3. Set the number of points you want the star to have, and then turn your attention to the Sharpness slider bar and text box (**Figure 10**). Play with the slider bar by moving the slider from right to left. Notice the change that sharpness has on the star in the preview pane.

4. When you are happy with the shape of the star, click OK.

5. With the Polygon Tool selected, press the left mouse button and drag it diagonally. The star will appear as you drag the mouse, becoming larger as you pull diagonally (**Figure 11**). Stars can be used for many types of drawings and borders (**Figures 12a–c**).

Create a Polygon as Star

With CorelDraw 7 you can create two types of spirals: symmetrical and logarithmic. The space between each revolution of a symmetrical spiral is the same, whereas the space between each revolution of a logarithmic spiral constantly increases.

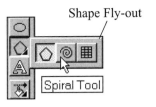

Figure 13. *The Spiral Tool is located on the Shape fly-out.*

To create a symmetrical spiral:

1. Click the little arrow on the Polygon Tool to open the Shape fly-out.

2. Select the Spiral Tool from the Shape fly-out (**Figure 13**). The mouse pointer will change to a cross-hair with a tiny spiral attached to it. The fly-out will close and the Spiral Tool button will replace the Polygon Tool button in the Toolbox (**Figure 14**).

Figure 14. *When the Spiral Tool is selected, its Toolbox button takes the place of the Polygon Tool button. To get the Polygon Tool button back, just select it from the Shape fly-out.*

3. Double-click on the Spiral Tool or right mouse click on the Spiral Tool and select Properties from the pop-up menu. The Options dialog box will open with the Toolbox tab to the front and Spiral Tool selected (**Figure 15**).

4. Select the Symmetrical option button as the Spiral tool default, and use the spin buttons to set the Number of revolutions (you can also type a number in the text box).

5. Click OK. The dialog box will close.

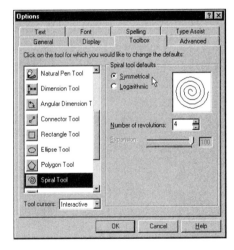

Figure 15. *Use the Spiral tool defaults area on the Toolbar tab page to change spiral default settings.*

Figure 16. *Drag the Spiral Tool diagonally to create a symmetrical spiral.*

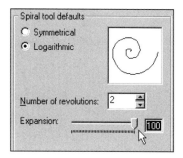

Figure 17. *Use the Spiral tool defaults area of the Toolbox tab page to select the Logarithmic spiral, Number of revolutions, and Expansion rate.*

Figure 18. *Drag the Spiral Tool diagonally to create a logarithmic spiral.*

6. With the Spiral Tool selected, press the left mouse button and drag it diagonally to create the symmetrical spiral (**Figure 16**). Release the mouse button when the spiral is the desired size.

To draw a logarithmic spiral:

1. Select the Spiral Tool from the Toolbox (**Figure 13**).

2. Double-click on the Spiral Tool to open the Options dialog box with the Toolbox tab page to the front and Spiral Tool selected (**Figure 15**).

2. In the Spiral tool defaults area, click the Logarithmic option button, set the Number of revolutions, and use the Expansion slider bar to set the expansion rate for each revolution of the spiral (**Figure 17**). As you move the slider, watch how the spiral expands in the preview pane.

3. Click OK when you are happy with the settings.

4. With the Spiral Tool selected, press the left mouse button and diagonally drag the tool to draw a logarithmic spiral (**Figure 18**).

5. Release the mouse button when the spiral is the right size.

Draw a Logarithmic Spiral

More about spirals:

■ You can draw spirals that rotate in a clockwise or counterclockwise direction, depending on which way you drag the mouse. If you drag the Spiral Tool diagonally up to the right, the spiral will rotate clockwise (**Figure 19**). If you drag the Spiral Tool diagonally down to the right, the spiral will rotate counter-clockwise (**Figure 20**).

■ You can add just a few lines to transform a spiral into something familiar (**Figure 21**).

Figure 19. *If you drag the Spiral Tool diagonally up to the right, the spiral will rotate clockwise.*

Figure 20. *If you drag the Spiral Tool diagonally down to the right, the spiral will rotate counterclockwise.*

Figure 21. *Adding a few lines to a spiral transforms it into something familiar.*

SUMMARY

In this chapter you learned how to:

■ Draw polygons

■ Change the number of sides of a polygon

■ Draw stars and polygons as stars

■ Adjust a star's sharpness

■ Change Spiral Tool default settings

■ Draw symmetrical and logarithmic spirals

More about Spirals

Nodes and Paths

T he *Shape Tool* (**Figure 1**) is used to manipulate an object's *nodes*. Nodes are the small, hollow squares that appear on an object's path right after the object is drawn or when it has been selected with the Shape Tool (**Figure 2**).

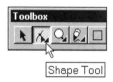

Figure 1. *The Shape Tool.*

Figure 2. *Nodes appear on an object's path when it is selected.*

Figure 3. *The mouse pointer changes to a large black arrowhead.*

These nodes may appear to be tiny squares of no consequence, but, in fact, they are very powerful. Nodes are used to manipulate specific line segments of an object's path. When you select the Shape Tool, the mouse pointer changes to a triangular, black arrowhead (**Figure 3**).

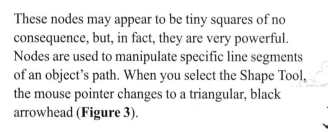

W̲hen you select an individual node with the Shape Tool, several things will happen: the node will change from hollow to black, and one or two *control points* attached to the node with *levers* will become visible (**Figure 4**). Control points determine the curvature of segments of a path. The levers are just a visual representation of which control point goes with which node. (You may have to zoom in to see this since these items are very small. For information on zooming in, see page 12.)

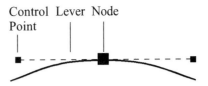

Figure 4. *When a node is selected with the Shape Tool, the node's control points become visible.*

There are three kinds of nodes:

- A *smooth* node is used to create a seamless curve. The control points of a smooth node are always directly opposite each other. If you were to move a control point, the opposite control point, which is locked into alignment with that control point, would move also. The distances between control points can vary (**Figure 5**). This means that the path on one side of a node can be curved differently than the path on the other side of the node.

Figure 5. *A smooth node's control points are locked into alignment, and the distances between the control points can vary.*

- A *symmetrical* node is very similar to a smooth node, in that its control points are always opposite each other and if you were to move a control point, the opposite control point would move also. What's different about a symmetrical node is that the control points are always the same distance from each other (**Figure 6**). This makes for a completely even shape on both sides of the node.

Figure 6. *A symmetrical node's control points are locked into alignment, and the control points are always the same distance apart.*

Smooth and Symmetrical Nodes

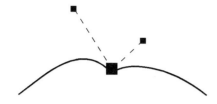

Figure 7. *A cusp node's control points move independently.*

Figure 8. *The selected node has no control points, therefore, the line that passes through it is straight.*

■ A *cusp* node is used to create sharp corners on a path. The cusp node's control points move independently of each other; thus, a curve that passes through a cusp node can bend at a sharp angle (**Figure 7**).

In order for a path segment to be bent, it must have control points. If a path segment is not bordered on either side by a control point, that path segment will be straight (**Figure 8**). A node can have from 0 to 2 control points.

A Rule of Thumb for Nodes

When you make changes to a node, the changes will affect the line segment located in a *counterclockwise* position from the node.

For instance, in the circle below (**Figure 9a**), the upper node is selected. When the Node roll-up is used to add a new node, the new node is added to the line segment located in a counterclockwise position from the selected node (**Figure 9b**).

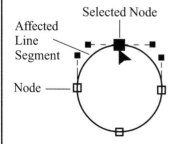

Figure 9a. *The circle's upper node is selected. Any changes will affect the line segment located in the counterclockwise position.*

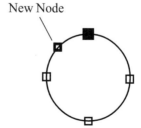

Figure 9b. *The new node is added to the counterclockwise line segment.*

Cusp Nodes

If you draw a shape such as a circle or rectangle, you will not be able to edit its nodes until you *convert the object to curves*.

To convert an object to curves:

1. Select the object using the Pick Tool.

2. Choose Convert To Curves from the Arrange menu (**Figure 10**) or press Ctrl+Q on the keyboard.

Tip:

■ Check the Status Bar to see if an object is already made up of curves or if it is a defined shape. If an object is a specific shape, the Status Bar will say something such as "Ellipse on Layer 1" or "Symmetrical Polygon with 10 sides on Layer 1" (**Figure 11**). If an object has been converted to curves, the Status Bar will display something such as "Curve on Layer 1" and will tell you how many nodes the object has (**Figure 12**).

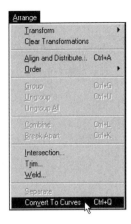

Figure 10. *Choose Convert to Curves from the Arrange menu to change a specific shape to an object comprised of curves.*

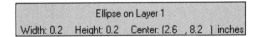

Figure 11. *The Status Bar will tell you whether you need to convert an object to curves. In this case, an elliptical shape is selected and the Status Bar states that this object is an "Ellipse on Layer 1."*

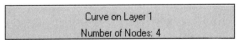

Figure 12. *After converting the elliptical shape to curves, the Status Bar states that the object is a "Curve on Layer 1."*

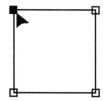

Figure 13. *Use the Shape Tool to click on the node you want to select.*

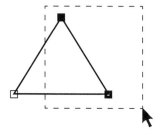

Figure 14. *You can marquee select several nodes at once.*

To select a node:

1. Select the object using the Shape Tool. The object's nodes will appear on the shape's path. (Check the Status Bar to make sure it says that the object is a curve. If it says the object is a rectangle or ellipse, for instance, you will have to *convert the object to curves*. See the previous page for more on how to do this.)

2. Select a node with the Shape Tool. The node will change from hollow to black (**Figure 13**).

To select multiple nodes:

1. Select the object with the Shape Tool.

2. Hold down the Shift key while clicking on the nodes you wish to select.

or

Press the left mouse button and drag the mouse. A dashed rectangle, or marquee, will appear as you drag. Release the mouse when the marquee encompasses the nodes you wish to select (**Figure 14**).

REMEMBER TO USE THE STATUS BAR

The Status Bar provides all sorts of useful information. If you want to know what kind of object or node you are looking at, select the item and take a look at the Status Bar.

Select a Node; Select Multiple Nodes

The Node Edit roll-up (**Figure 15**) is used to edit the properties of nodes and paths. When a node is changed, it alters the shape of the path passing through the node. For instance, suppose there were two lines you wanted to connect. You would use the Node Edit roll-up to join the nodes at the end of each line.

Figure 15. *You can use the Node Edit roll-up to change node properties.*

With all its buttons, the Node Edit roll-up may look confusing at first, but don't let that deter you! As you make your way through this chapter, it will become a familiar tool.

Sometimes you will encounter a node with no control points (**Figure 16**). This is because the path that is passing through the node is a perfectly straight line segment. To add control points to such a node, you will need to *convert the line to curves*.

Figure 16. *The selected node has no control points, therefore the line is perfectly straight.*

To add control points to a node or make a straight line curved:

1. Use the Shape Tool to double-click on the node with no control points. This will select the node and open the Node Edit roll-up.

2. Click the Convert Line to Curve button (**Figure 17**). Control points will appear, bordering each side of the line segment (**Figure 18**), one on the selected node and the other on the node located in a counterclockwise position from the selected node.

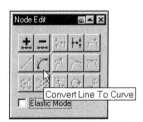

Figure 17. *Press the Convert Line to Curve button to add a control point to a node.*

Figure 18. *After pressing the Convert Line to Curve button, control points appear bordering the line segment.*

The Node Edit Roll-up; Add Control Points

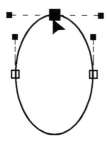

Figure 19. *Use the Shape Tool to select the node you want to convert.*

Figure 20. *Press the Convert Curve to Line button to make a curved line straight.*

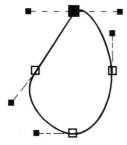

Figure 21. *When the curved line is converted to a straight one, the control points bordering each side of the line disappear.*

To make a curved line segment perfectly straight, you will have to do the opposite of converting a line to curves—you will need to *convert a curve to a line*.

To make a curved line straight:

1. Use the Shape Tool to double-click on the node you want to convert to select the node and open the Node Edit roll-up (**Figure 19**).

2. Press the Convert Curve to Line button (**Figure 20**).

3. The control points will disappear and the line will become straight (**Figure 21**).

SWITCH BETWEEN TOOLS

To quickly switch between the tool you are using and the Pick Tool, press the space bar on your keyboard. To return to the other tool, press the space bar again.

Make a Curved Line Straight

Special Project:

Create a Heart

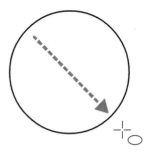

Figure 22. *Hold down the Ctrl key while using the Ellipse Tool to draw a perfect circle.*

Changing a circle into a heart is easy to do. Follow the steps to discover how to create a heart by converting nodes from one type to another, moving control points to achieve the desired curve, and moving the nodes themselves to stretch path segments.

To start the heart:

1. Draw a perfect circle using the Ellipse Tool while holding down the Ctrl key (**Figure 22**).

2. Convert the circle to curves by either pressing Ctrl+Q on the keyboard or choosing Convert To Curves on the Arrange menu.

3. Select the object with the Shape Tool to display its nodes (**Figure 23**).

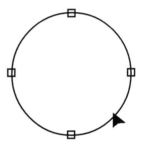

Figure 23. *Use the Shape Tool to select the object and display its nodes.*

4. Use the Shape Tool to select the node at the bottom of the circle. When you do, several control points appear (**Figure 24**) at the bottom and sides. If you look at the Status Bar, you will see that the node you have selected is a "Curve Symmetrical"—meaning, a symmetrical node. The bottom of a heart is pointed, so you are going to have to convert the symmetrical node to a cusp node to achieve the point.

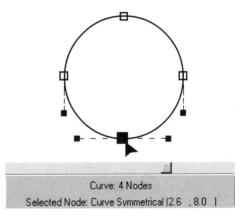

Curve: 4 Nodes
Selected Node: Curve Symmetrical (2.6 , 8.0)

Figure 24. *When you select the bottom node, the Status Bar tells you what type of node it is.*

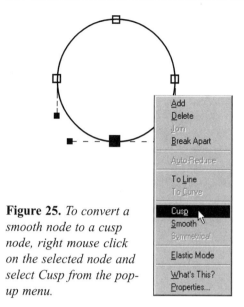

Figure 25. *To convert a smooth node to a cusp node, right mouse click on the selected node and select Cusp from the pop-up menu.*

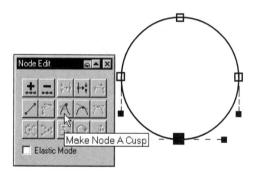

Figure 26. *Click the Make Node A Cusp button to convert the node.*

To convert a smooth node to a cusp node:

1. Use the Shape Tool to select the node you want to convert.

2. Position the pointer on the selected node and right mouse click to open the pop-up menu and select Cusp (**Figure 25**).

or

1. Double-click on the node with the Shape Tool. This will select the node and open the Node Edit roll-up.

2. Click the button in the very center of the roll-up to convert the symmetrical node to a cusp node (**Figure 26**). (Thankfully, ToolTips help will display to tell you which button is the Make Node A Cusp button!)

Tip:

■ Use either of the procedures above to convert any type of node to another type—for instance, you could convert a smooth node to a symmetrical node.

Convert a Smooth Node to a Cusp Node

USE THE KEYBOARD TO OPEN THE NODE EDIT ROLL-UP

To quickly open the Node Edit roll-up, press Ctrl+F10 on your keyboard.

Next, to make the circle look more like a heart, you will need to move the bottom node down a little to elongate the sides of the circle.

To move a node:

1. Select the node with the Shape Tool.
2. Press the left mouse button and drag until you are satisfied with the shape (**Figure 27**).
3. Release the mouse button.

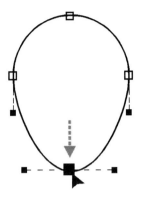

Figure 27. *Press the left mouse button and drag the node to the desired position.*

The next step is to move the node's control points upward to create the heart's point at the bottom of the circle.

To move a control point:

1. Select the node you want to edit with the Shape Tool.
2. Move the tip of the Shape Tool arrow to the control point you want to move.
3. Press the left mouse button and drag the control point until you have achieved the desired curve (**Figure 28**).

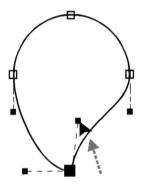

Figure 28. *Drag the control point until you have achieved the desired curve.*

To create the heart's point, both the right and left control points at the bottom of the circle should be stretched up to create the point (**Figure 29**).

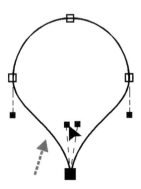

Figure 29. *To create the heart's bottom point, drag the control points upward.*

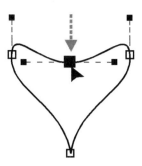

Figure 30. *Drag the cusp node down to shape the top of the heart.*

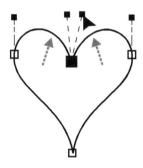

Figure 31. *Drag the control points up to create the heart's sharp angle.*

Finishing the heart is easy. All you have to do is apply what you have learned to the node at the top of the circle. Look at the shape of the top of the circle. What shape do you need there to create a heart? The top of a heart has a sharp dimple—an angle—so you are going to need a cusp node.

To create the top of the heart:

1. Convert the symmetrical node at the top of the circle to a cusp node.

2. Move the cusp node down, using the Shape Tool, to begin shaping the top of the heart (**Figure 30**).

3. Next, drag and stretch the cusp node's control points up to create the sharp angle and rounded tops of the heart (**Figure 31**). *Voilà!* Hearts can be used in many kinds of drawings (**Figures 32a–d**).

Figures 32a–d.

Finish the Heart

To manually add a node to a path:

1. Select the object using the Shape Tool.

2. Click on the path where you want to add the node. A circular, temporary node will appear on the line segment (**Figure 33**).

3. With the Shape Tool's pointer positioned over the temporary node, right mouse click and select Add from the pop-up menu (**Figure 34**) or press the ⊞ key on your keypad.

or

1. Double-click with the Shape Tool on the path where you want to add the node. A circular, temporary node will appear on the path and the Node Edit roll-up will open.

2. Click the Add Node(s) button on the roll-up (**Figure 35**).

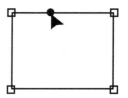

Figure 33. *Use the Shape Tool to click on the path where you want to add a node.*

Figure 34. *Select Add from the pop-up menu.*

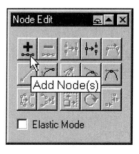

Figure 35. *Press the Add Node(s) button on the Node Edit roll-up.*

Manually Add a Node to a Path

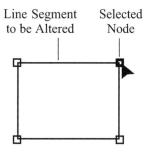

Line Segment to be Altered   Selected Node

Figure 36. *Select the node that is positioned clockwise to the line segment that you want to alter.*

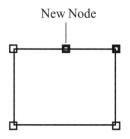

New Node

Figure 37. *The new node appears at the center of the line segment.*

To automatically add a node to a line segment:

1. Select the node whose position is clockwise to the line segment you want to edit (**Figure 36**).

2. Press Ctrl+F10 on the keyboard to open the Node Edit roll-up.

3. Click the Add Node(s) button on the roll-up (**Figure 35**). A new node will appear, selected, that evenly divides the path into two segments (**Figure 37**).

Tip:

■   The type of node you select before pressing the Add Node(s) button determines what type of node will be added. For instance, if you select a cusp node then press the Add Node(s) button, a new cusp node will be added to the path.

TOOLTIPS AND THE NODE EDIT ROLL-UP

There are so many buttons on the Node Edit roll-up that it can look rather confusing. Remember that ToolTips help is always available. To make sure the ToolTips help balloon will display, click on the roll-up to make it active. As you slowly pass the mouse pointer over the different buttons, small balloons will appear, describing what each button does. Figure 35 shows the ToolTip that appears when the mouse is passed over the Add Node(s) button.

Automatically Add a Node to a Path

To delete a node from a path:

1. Select the node you want to delete using the Shape Tool.

2. With the Shape Tool's pointer positioned over the selected node, right mouse click and choose Delete from the pop-up menu (**Figure 38**) or press the Delete key on your keyboard.

or

1. Choose the node you want to delete using the Shape Tool.

2. Double-click on the node you want to delete. The Node Edit roll-up will appear.

3. Click the Delete Node(s) button on the roll-up (**Figure 39**).

Tips:

■ Several nodes can be deleted at once by multiply selecting them and using either of the above methods.

■ You can also delete a node by selecting it then pressing the ⊟ key on your keypad.

■ If you try to delete a node by selecting it then pressing the Backspace key, your computer will beep and nothing will happen.

Figure 38. *After selecting the node you want to delete, click the right mouse button and choose Delete from the pop-up menu.*

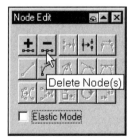

Figure 39. *You can also use the Node Edit roll-up to delete nodes.*

Delete a Node From a Path

Figure 40. *After selecting the node you want to break into two, right mouse click and choose Break Apart from the pop-up menu.*

Figure 41. *A broken curve contains two nodes, one on top of the other. Move one of the nodes away using the Shape Tool.*

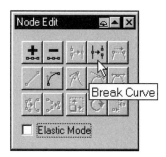

Figure 42. *You can also use the Node Edit roll-up to break apart a curve or node.*

To break a curve or break apart a node:

1. With the Shape Tool, select the node where you want to break the curve.

2. Position the Shape Tool's pointer over the selected node and right mouse click. Choose Break Apart from the pop-up menu (**Figure 40**). There are now two nodes where there was one.

3. Use the Shape Tool to move one of the nodes off the other (**Figure 41**).

or

1. Use the Shape Tool to double-click on the node you want to break into two. The Node Edit roll-up will open on your screen.

2. Click the Break Curve button on the roll-up (**Figure 42**).

Tip:

■ If you break apart the path of a closed object that is filled with color—a circle, for instance—the color will disappear because the path is now open.

Break Apart a Node

To join two nodes into one:

1. Select one node by double-clicking on it. This will open the Node Edit roll-up at the same time.

2. Press Shift and then click and select the second node that you want to join to the first (**Figure 43**).

3. Click the Join Two Nodes button on the Node Edit roll-up (**Figure 44a**). The two nodes will move together and become one (**Figure 44b**).

To join two nodes with a straight line:

1. Open the Node Edit roll-up by pressing Ctrl+F10 on the keyboard.

2. Select the two nodes you want to join with a line (**Figure 43**).

3. Click the Extend Curve to Close button (**Figure 45a**). A straight line will appear, joining the two nodes (**Figure 45b**).

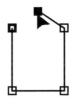

Figure 43. *Use the Shape Tool to select the two nodes you want to join.*

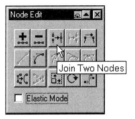

Figure 44a. *Click the Join Two Nodes button to join the two selected nodes into one.*

Figure 44b. *When the Join Two Nodes button is pressed, the line segments attached to those nodes move together.*

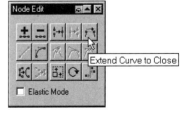

Figure 45a. *Click the Extend Curve to Close button to add a line that joins the two nodes.*

Figure 45b. *After the Extend Curve to Close button is pressed, a straight line appears, joining the two selected nodes.*

Join Nodes; Join Nodes with a Straight Line

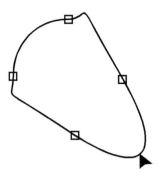

Figure 46. *Use the Shape Tool to drag a path and change its shape.*

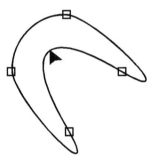

Figure 47. *As you drag a path, the object's nodes will remain stationary. The shape of each path segment will change, depending upon the node type that it passes through.*

n object's path can also be manipulated without using nodes.

To directly manipulate an object's path:

1. Select the object using the Shape Tool. (If the Status Bar says that the object is a specific shape, not a curve with nodes, you will have to convert the object to curves.)

2. Place the pointer of the Shape Tool on the object's path, press the left mouse button, and drag the mouse (**Figure 46**). As you drag, notice that stretching the line segment also affects the rest of the object—the nodes stay stationary while the line segments stretch and curve according to the node type they pass through (**Figure 47**).

3. When you are happy with the shape, release the mouse button (**Figure 48**). A simple dot and curved line brings the shape to life (**Figure 49**).

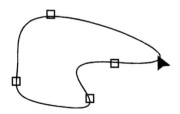

Figure 48. *The object's new shape.*

Figure 49. *A dot and curved line adds personality.*

Directly Manipulate a Path

Special Project:

Make Waves

Figure 50. *Draw a perfect circle by holding down the Ctrl key while dragging the Ellipse Tool.*

I t's time to take what you have learned and create something fun. The wave shape is easy to make and can be used in many drawings, including seagulls and house roofs (check out the town scene on page 59).

Figure 51. *Select the converted circle with the Shape Tool.*

To create waves:

1. Draw a perfect circle using the Ellipse Tool while holding down the Ctrl key (**Figure 50**).

2. Convert the circle to curves by either selecting Convert To Curves from the Arrange menu or pressing Ctrl+Q on the keyboard.

3. Select the circle using the Shape Tool. Four nodes will become visible around the circle (**Figure 51**).

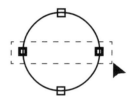

Figure 52. *Use the Shape Tool to marquee select the left and right nodes.*

4. Marquee select the nodes on the right and left sides of the circle (**Figure 52**).

5. With the Shape Tool's pointer positioned over one of the selected nodes, right mouse click and select Break Apart from the pop-up menu (**Figure 53**).

Figure 53. *Place the Shape Tool pointer on one of the selected nodes and right click. Choose Break Apart on the pop-up menu.*

Figure 54. *Select Break Apart from the Arrange menu.*

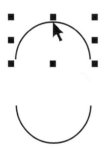

Figure 55. *Select the upper arc and drag it up and away from the lower arc.*

Figure 56. *After you delete the top arc, the bottom arc is left.*

Figure 57. *Hold down the right mouse button to drag a copy of the arc.*

6. Select Break Apart from the Arrange menu (**Figure 54**) or press Ctrl+K on the keyboard. This will break the circle into two halves—an upper and a lower.

7. Switch to the Pick Tool and position the pointer on the path at the top of the broken circle. Press the left mouse button and drag it up. When you release the mouse, the upper arc will be selected (**Figure 55**).

8. Press the Delete key on the keyboard to delete the top half of the circle. You will be left with the bottom half—the left side of a wave (**Figure 56**).

9. Press the right mouse button and the Ctrl key and drag a copy of the half circle over to the right, positioning the left tip of the new arc on top of the right tip of the first arc (**Figure 57**).

Special Project: Make Waves

10. Release the mouse button and Ctrl key and select Copy Here from the pop-up menu that appears (**Figure 58**). You've made your first wave! (**Figure 59**)

Figure 58. *Release the mouse button and select Copy Here from the pop-up menu.*

11. Marquee select the entire wave and use the drag-copy procedure a few more times to make more waves (**Figure 60**). You can use these same techniques to create more complex waves, such as those shown at the bottom of this page.

Figure 59. *Copy the arc to create your first wave.*

Figure 60. *It's easy to make an ocean of waves.*

SUMMARY

In this chapter you learned how to:

- Convert an object to curves
- Convert a line to curves
- Convert a curve to a line
- Select nodes

- Convert node types
- Move, add, and delete nodes
- Break a node into two
- Join two nodes together
- Make waves

*C*orelDraw 7 offers three tools for drawing lines and curves: the Freehand, Bézier, and Natural Pen Tools. You can find them on the Curve fly-out (**Figure 1**).

Curve Fly-out

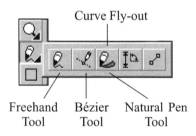

Freehand Tool · Bézier Tool · Natural Pen Tool

Figure 1. *The Curve fly-out.*

Of the three, the Freehand Tool is the most straightforward because it works like a pencil on paper. As you drag the Freehand Tool, it creates curves and lines, mirroring the motions of the mouse.

The Bézier Tool draws on a node-by-node basis. As you learned in the last chapter, nodes control the curve of the line segment that passes through them. With the Bézier Tool you can draw smooth, accurate curves node-by-node. With each click of the mouse a node is created and each node is connected to the previous node by a line segment.

The Natural Pen Tool is a new CorelDraw 7 feature. With it you can draw lines of varying thicknesses. It works just like the Freehand Tool because you drag it to draw. However, instead of creating a single, thick outline, it actually creates an object made up of a closed path.

The Freehand Tool is easy to use and will probably feel familiar to you right from the start. At first, your lines may appear rough, but you can always refine them using their nodes and the Shape Tool. As you continue to practice with the Freehand Tool, drawing will come quite naturally.

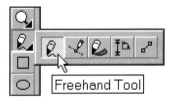

Figure 2. *Select the Freehand Tool from the Curve fly-out.*

To draw a straight line:

1. Select the Freehand Tool (**Figure 2**). The mouse pointer will change to a cross-hair with a little squiggle attached to it.

2. Click on the place where you want the line to begin.

3. Click on the place where you want the line to end (**Figure 3**).

Figure 3. *Click where you want the line to begin, then click where you want the line to end.*

To constrain (force) a straight line to an angle:

1. Select the Freehand Tool, click on the place where you want the line to start, and hold down the Ctrl key.

2. Move the mouse to where you want the line to end. Notice that as you move the mouse around, the line moves in 15° increments (**Figure 4**).

3. Click on the place where you want the line to end, then release the Ctrl key.

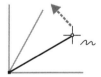

Figure 4. *Hold the Ctrl key down to constrain the line to 15° increments.*

Tip:

■ Keep an eye on the Status Bar as you draw the line. It will tell you what angle the line is at.

Figure 5. *Drag the mouse to draw a curve.*

Figure 6. *When you are finished drawing, release the mouse. Several nodes will appear along the length of the curve.*

WHY ARE THERE MORE NODES AT ONE END OF THE CURVE THAN THE OTHER?

As you draw a curve with the Free-hand Tool, CorelDraw automatically places nodes along the curve. The faster you move the mouse, the fewer nodes will appear along the path. If you slow down while drawing, CorelDraw is programed to add extra nodes. It assumes that you are trying to emphasize that part of the curve. Remember that if there are too many nodes on a curve section, you can delete them using the Shape Tool.

To draw a curved line:

1. Select the Freehand Tool from the Toolbox.

2. Position the Freehand Tool to where you want the curve to start.

3. Press the left mouse button and drag it, like you would a pencil on paper, to create the curve (**Figure 5**).

4. Release the mouse when you are finished. CorelDraw will smooth the curve shape and several nodes will appear along the path (**Figure 6**).

To erase part of a line as you draw:

1. Without releasing the mouse button and discontinuing the line you are drawing, hold down the Shift key.

2. Drag the Freehand Tool backwards along the line that you've already drawn.

3. Release the Shift key when you have finished erasing (but don't release the mouse button) and resume drawing the line.

To create a closed object:

Use the Freehand Tool to create the shape you desire, making sure that the line segments begin and end at the same point.

Draw a Curved Line; Erase Part of a Line

W ith the Bézier Tool, you can draw smooth curves very precisely, node-by-node. As each node is created, you can control how curvy a line is by manipulating the node's control points.

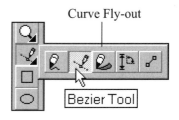

Curve Fly-out

Figure 7. *Select the Bézier Tool from the Curve fly-out.*

To draw a straight line:

1. Select the Bézier Tool from the Curve fly-out (**Figure 7**). The mouse pointer will change to a cross-hair with a tiny curve connected to it.

2. Click on the place where you want to position the first node.

3. Click where you want to place the second node. A straight line segment will appear between the two nodes (**Figure 8**).

Figure 8. *Click where you want the line to begin, then click again where you want the line to end.*

Tip:

■ Press the Spacebar twice, or select another tool, to stop drawing with the Bézier Tool.

To create a closed object:

Select the Bézier Tool and click to add nodes and create the shape you desire. To close the object, make sure the last click of the mouse is positioned directly on top of the first node you placed.

WHO WAS BÉZIER ANYHOW?

The Bézier curve—the curve representation used most frequently in computer graphics—is named after Pierre Bézier, a French engineer who worked for the car manufacturer Renault. In the 1960s, in an attempt to draw car parts, he developed the mathematical equations that represent a curve geometrically.

Bézier Tool: Draw a Straight Line

Figure 9. *After selecting the Bézier Tool, press the left mouse button and drag to create a node with two control points.*

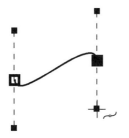

Figure 10. *Press and drag the mouse again to add a second node and create a curve.*

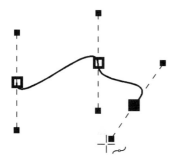

Figure 11. *Press and drag the mouse a third time to add another node and curve.*

To create a curve:

1. Select the Bézier Tool from the Curve fly-out.

2. Position the Bézier Tool where you want to start the curve, press the left mouse button, and drag the mouse. A node will appear with two control points that stretch in opposite positions as you drag the mouse (**Figure 9**).

3. Release the mouse when the control points are the desired distance from the node.

4. Move the mouse to the place where you want to position the next node. Press and drag the mouse to create another node with two control points. A curved line segment will appear between the two nodes (**Figure 10**). If you want to add another node to continue the curve, repeat this step again (**Figure 11**). If you want to stop adding nodes to this curve, press the Spacebar twice.

Tips:

■ To create a node with one control point, click to create the node, then position the mouse over the node, press the left mouse button and drag.

■ To create a node with no control points, just click (don't drag).

■ The distance between a node and its control points determines how curved the line segment will be. The further away the control points are from the node, the deeper the curve will be.

Create a Curved Line

Special Project:

Draw a Flag

Figure 12. *Select the Bézier Tool, then press and drag the mouse diagonally up to the left.*

*I*t's time to take the skills you have learned and use them to create an object. Check out the flags on page 79. They use Bézier curves to create the look of flags flying in the breeze.

To draw a flag:

1. Use the Zoom Box on the Standard Toolbar to zoom in to 200% and then select the Bézier Tool.

2. Position the pointer where you want the top left corner of the flag to be. Press the mouse button and drag it up diagonally to the left (**Figure 12**). Release the mouse.

3. Move the pointer to the right about 1 inch (2.5 centimeters) and press and drag the mouse down diagonally to the left (**Figure 13**).

Figure 13. *Press the mouse again and drag the control point down and to the left.*

4. Continue pressing the mouse while you drag that new control point up to the right (**Figure 14**). This will press the curve down, making it dip. Release the mouse.

5. Position the mouse pointer again to the right about 1 inch. This node will create the upper right corner of the flag. Press the mouse and drag it up diagonally to the right (**Figure 15**), then release the mouse.

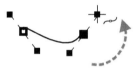

Figure 14. *Continue pressing the mouse and swing the control point around up to the right.*

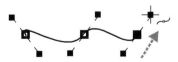

Figure 15. *Create another node by pressing the mouse and dragging diagonally up to the right.*

Special Project: Draw a Flag

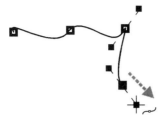

Figure 16. *Create a fourth node about an inch below the third node by pressing the mouse and dragging diagonally down to the right.*

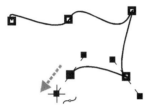

Figure 17. *Press and drag the mouse down and to the left.*

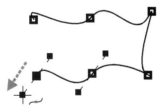

Figure 18. *Create the next node by pressing and dragging the mouse down to the left again.*

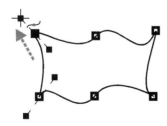

Figure 19. *Close the object by positioning the mouse over the first node and pressing and dragging the mouse up to the left.*

6. Move the mouse pointer down about an inch below the node you just created. Press the mouse button and drag it diagonally down to the right (**Figure 16**) and release the mouse. You've just created the right side of the flag.

7. Position the mouse about an inch to the left of that node and press and drag the mouse down diagonally to the left (**Figure 17**), then release the mouse. This will make the curve mirror the one above it.

8. Move the mouse again one inch to the left and press and drag it diagonally down to the left (**Figure 18**) to mirror the curve that is above it. Release the mouse.

9. Position the cursor on top of the first node you created, then press and drag the mouse up diagonally to the left (**Figure 19**) to close the object. Release the mouse and press the Spacebar twice to stop drawing with the Bézier Tool.

10. Add stars and lines as you desire (see Chapter 5 for drawing stars). You could even use the Rectangle and Ellipse Tools to create a flag pole (**Figure 20**).

Figure 20. *It's easy to make a waving flag.*

Special Project: Draw a Flag

*C*reating lines and curves is just the beginning! Using the Outline Tool fly-out (**Figure 21**) and the Pen roll-up (**Figure 22**), you can make your lines thicker, change their style from solid to dashed or dotted, and give them a calligraphic look.

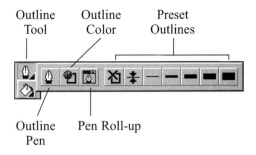

Figure 21. *The Outline Tool fly-out.*

The Outline Tool fly-out

As you may have already noticed, the last two buttons on the CorelDraw 7 toolbar are separated from the rest by a space. This is because these two buttons, the Outline and Fill Tools, work differently from their neighbors. Instead of being tools that are used for drawing, such as the Rectangle Tool, these two buttons access fly-outs that change the appearance of a drawing. This chapter will make full use of the Outline Tool and its fly-out (**Figure 21**). The Fill Tool will be discussed later in Chapter 10, *Color and Fills*. To access the Outline Tool fly-out, just click the Outline Tool button.

The Pen roll-up

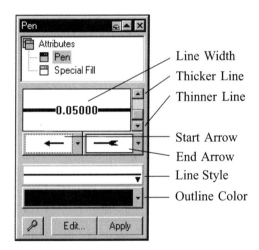

Figure 22. *The Pen roll-up.*

The Pen roll-up (**Figure 22**) is used to change the properties of the lines that you draw with the Freehand and Bézier Tools and the outlines of the objects you draw with the Rectangle, Ellipse, and Polygon Tools.

The Outline Tool; the Pen Roll-up

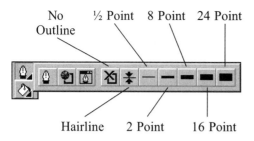

No Outline   ½ Point   8 Point   24 Point

Hairline   2 Point   16 Point

Figure 23. *The Outline Tool fly-out contains several preset line widths.*

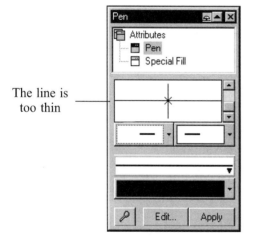

The line is too thin

Figure 24. *If the line width is set too thin, an X will appear in the Line Width view pane.*

To change line thickness:

1. Click the Outline Tool to open the fly-out.

2. Click one of the preset outline width buttons (**Figure 23**).

or

1. Open the Outline Tool fly-out and select the Pen Roll-up button (**Figure 21**). The Pen roll-up will open.

2. Use the up and down scroll bar arrows near the middle of the Pen roll-up to increase or decrease the line thickness (**Figure 22**). As you click the arrows, the Line Width view pane will give you a preview of the line width.

3. Click Apply.

Tip:

■   If the line width is set to 0.003 inch (0.216 point) or thinner, an X will appear in the Line Width view pane (**Figure 24**). This means that the outline is too thin and may not print well.

■   If your object is not filled with a color and you click the No Outline button, the object's outline will disappear and you may lose track of the object!

Change Line Thickness

To change the line style:

1. Select the object you want to change with the Pick Tool.

2. Click on the Outline Tool button to open the fly-out and then click the Pen roll-up button (**Figure 21**) to open the roll-up.

3. Click the down arrow in the Line Style box (**Figure 25**).

4. Move your mouse down the list that appears until you find the line style you want, then click that one (**Figure 26**). The drop-down list will close and the line style you selected will appear in the line style box.

5. Click Apply.

To add arrowheads to a line:

1. Select the line with the Pick Tool.

2. Open the Pen roll-up by clicking on the Outline Tool to open the fly-out and then clicking the Pen roll-up button.

3. Use the Start Arrow and End Arrow drop-down lists to select arrow styles (**Figure 27**).

4. Click the Apply button when you have selected both a Start Arrow and an End Arrow.

Tip:

■ Check out the options available on the Start Arrow and End Arrow drop-down lists. You'll be surprised at what you find there (**Figures 28a–c**).

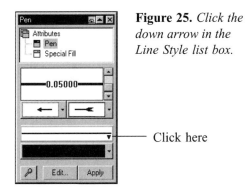

Figure 25. *Click the down arrow in the Line Style list box.*

Click here

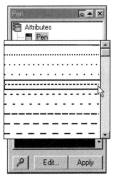

Figure 26. *Choose the line style you want from the list that appears.*

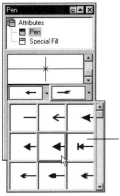

Figure 27. *Use the Start Arrow drop-down list to select an arrow style. Do the same with the End Arrow drop-down list.*

Start Arrow Drop-down List

Figures 28a–c. *There are many arrowheads from which to choose.*

Figure 29. *Select the line you want to alter with the Pick Tool.*

Figure 30. *Open the Outline Pen dialog box by clicking the Outline Pen button.*

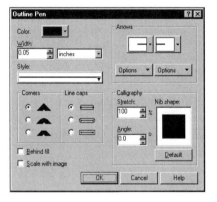

Figure 31. *The Outline Pen dialog box.*

Figure 32. *Select a nib shape by choosing one of the Corner Styles.*

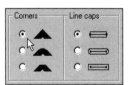

Figure 33. *Set the Stretch and Angle of the nib in the Calligraphy area.*

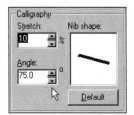

To give a line the appearance of calligraphy:

1. Select the line you want to alter with the Pick Tool (**Figure 29**).

2. Open the Outline Tool fly-out and click the Outline Pen button (**Figure 30**). The Outline Pen dialog box will open (**Figure 31**).

3. Select a Corner style (**Figure 32**). The top and bottom styles, Miter and Bevel, respectively, will create a square *nib* shape. (A nib is the point of a calligraphy pen.) The middle style, Rounded, will create a round nib shape.

4. In the Calligraphy area, set the nib's Stretch and Angle using the available text boxes (**Figure 33**). The Stretch setting determines how square or round the nib will be. The lower the setting, the thinner the nib and the more variation there will be in drawn line thickness.

5. Click OK. The line will be reshaped and look like it was drawn with a calligraphy pen (**Figure 34**). Notice the variation in the line thickness.

Figure 34. *When you click OK the line is transformed.*

Create Calligraphy Lines

89

*N*ew to CorelDraw 7, the Natural Pen Tool lets you quickly draw closed paths that look like thick lines and curves. This tool offers several interesting drawing modes: Fixed Width, Pressure, Calligraphy, and Preset.

Drawing with the Natural Pen Tool is like drawing with the Freehand Tool. All you need to do is press the mouse and drag. A line will appear as your mouse moves. At first, your drawings may appear rough, but with practice they will quickly become professional.

To access the different modes of the Natural Pen Tool:

1. Select the Natural Pen Tool from the Curve fly-out (**Figure 35**).

2. Click one of the four buttons on the Property Bar near the top of the screen (**Figure 36**). Each Natural Pen mode produces different effects (**Figure 37**).

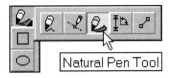

Figure 35. *Select the Natural Pen Tool from the Curve fly-out.*

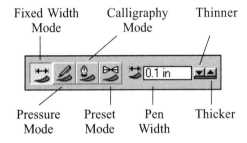

Figure 36. *There are four Natural Pen Tool drawing modes. You can access them by clicking the appropriate button on the Property Bar.*

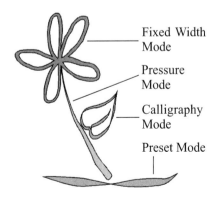

Figure 37. *The four Natural Pen Tool modes produce very different effects.*

Figure 38. *As you drag the mouse a thick line appears.*

Figure 39. *When you release the mouse, the outline of the curve remains.*

Calligraphy Mode   Pen Width   Nib Angle

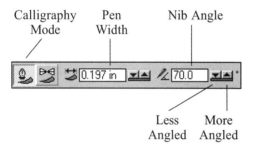

Less Angled   More Angled

Figure 40. *After selecting the Calligraphy drawing mode, set the nib angle.*

Figure 41. *Drag the mouse to create the calligraphic curve.*

Figure 42. *When you release the mouse, the curve outline remains.*

*T*he Fixed Width mode of the Natural Pen Tool will draw a curve that is the same thickness along its entire length.

To draw a Fixed Width curve:

1. Select the Natural Pen Tool from the Curve fly-out (**Figure 35**). The mouse pointer will change to a cross-hair with a little squiggle attached to it.

2. Use the Property Bar to select the Fixed Width mode button (**Figure 36**). You can also set the width of the curve using the text box and arrows next to the Natural Pen Tool buttons.

3. Press the left mouse button and drag (**Figure 38**). When you release the mouse button the outline of the curve will appear (**Figure 39**).

*T*he Calligraphy mode is easy to use. All you have to do is set the nib angle.

To draw a Calligraphy curve:

1. Select the Natural Pen Tool, then click the Calligraphy mode button on the Property Bar (**Figure 40**).

2. Use the text box and arrows to set the nib angle.

3. Press the left mouse button and drag (**Figure 41**). When you release the mouse an outline of the calligraphy curve will appear (**Figure 42**).

Fixed Width Mode; Calligraphy Mode

The Pressure drawing mode works with either a pressure-sensitive pen or the up or down arrows on the keyboard.

To draw using the Pressure mode:

1. Select the Natural Pen Tool, then click the Pressure mode button on the Property Bar (**Figure 36**).

2. Press the left mouse button and drag. Use the up arrow on the keyboard to apply more pressure and make the line thicker (**Figure 43**). Use the down arrow to make the line thinner. If you are using a pressure pen or stylus, the line will get thicker when you press harder and thinner when you press less hard.

The Preset mode uses predefined nib shapes to create interesting curves.

To draw using the Preset mode:

1. Select the Natural Pen Tool, then click the Preset mode button on the Property Bar (**Figure 44**).

2. Select a preset nib from the drop-down list (**Figure 44**), then press and drag the mouse. When you release the mouse, your curve will take on the shape of the nib (**Figure 45**).

Figure 43. *As you drag the mouse, press the up arrow key on the keyboard to make the line thicker. If you press the down arrow key, the line will get thinner.*

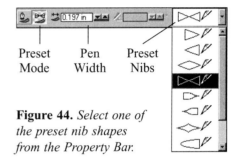

Preset Mode · Pen Width · Preset Nibs

Figure 44. *Select one of the preset nib shapes from the Property Bar.*

Figure 45. *When you draw a line and release the mouse button, that line will assume the preset nib shape.*

SUMMARY

In this chapter you learned how to:

- ■ Draw lines
- ■ Draw curves
- ■ Create closed objects
- ■ Erase part of a line
- ■ Create a flag
- ■ Change line thickness

Page and Document Setup

Besides being a versatile drawing tool, CorelDraw 7 includes expanded desktop publishing capabilities. This means that you can use CorelDraw 7 to create many types of multiple-page publications such as brochures, flyers, and catalogs. (Formerly, this required separate desktop publishing software.) In addition, you can create documents for any paper size that is used anywhere in the world.

In this chapter you will learn how to set page size and orientation and set the default unit of measure. From there you will add and remove pages from a document and find out how to quickly move between pages. Then, you will display a document in two windows and see how easy it is to edit a drawing up close in one window while viewing the entire drawing in the other. Finally, you will view two different documents at the same time and use drag-and-drop to move or copy items from one document to another.

Desktop Publishing: Folding Styles

DESKTOP PUBLISHING FOLDING STYLES

Printers use special terms for the way paper is folded. Below are a few standard folding styles:

Full Page   Booklet   Tent Fold   Side Fold   Top Fold

To select a page size and orientation:

1. From the Layout menu, choose Page Setup (**Figure 1**). This will open the Layout dialog box (**Figure 2**).

2. In the Paper size area at the top left of the dialog box, click the arrow next to the Paper list box to display the predefined paper sizes (**Figure 3**). Select the paper size that you want. If you don't remember how large a particular predefined page size is, just select it. Its dimensions will be displayed automatically in the Width and Height text boxes.

3. Use the option buttons next to Portrait and Landscape to select a page orientation, then click OK.

Tip:

- To specify a paper size that is not predefined, set the page dimensions using the Width and Height text boxes.

- Check out the "Labels" item in the Paper list box. There are hundreds of predefined labels, categorized by manufacturer—Ace, Avery, Nashua, and Nebs, to name a few—and manufacturer's stock number.

Figure 1. *Select Page Setup from the Layout menu.*

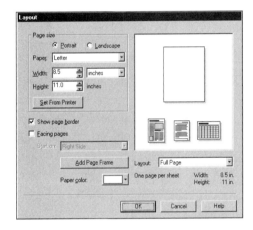

Figure 2. *The Layout dialog box is used to select page size and orientation.*

Figure 3. *Select a paper size from the Paper list box.*

WHICH WAY IS MY PAGE ORIENTED?

The term *page orientation* refers to the way a page is situated. If the page is taller than it is wide, it is in *portrait* orientation (**Figure 4**). If the page is wider than it is tall, it is in *landscape* orientation (**Figure 5**).

Figure 4. *This is a portrait page.*

Figure 5. *This is a landscape page.*

WHAT'S IN A UNIT OF MEASURE?

There are many units of measure in use in the desktop publishing world including inches, centimeters, picas, and points. Here's how some of the standard units measure up:

Unit	1 Inch =
Centimeters	2.54 centimeters
Picas	6 picas
Points	72 points

Page Orientation; Measurement Units

To change the unit of measure:

1. Open the Layout dialog box by selecting Page Setup on the Layout menu.

2. In the Paper size area at the top left of the dialog box, use the list box next to the Width text box to select a new measurement system (**Figure 6**).

3. Click OK.

Figure 6. *You can use the list box next to the Width text box to select the unit of measure.*

or

1. Select Grid and Ruler Setup from the Layout menu (**Figure 7**). The Grid & Ruler dialog box will open with the Ruler tab page in front (**Figure 8**).

2. In the Units area at the top of the tab page, use the list boxes found to the right of Horizontal and Vertical to select a new measurement unit. (Be sure the box next to "Same units for Horizontal and Vertical rulers" is checked, otherwise the rulers will display different measurement units.)

3. Click OK.

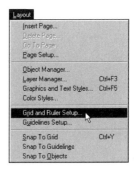

Figure 7. *Select Grid and Ruler Setup from the Layout menu.*

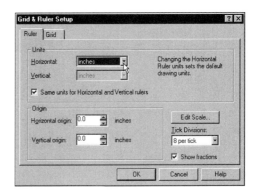

Figure 8. *Use the Ruler tab page of the Grid & Ruler Setup dialog box to set a measurement system.*

Change the Unit of Measure

Figure 9. *Select Insert Page from the Layout menu.*

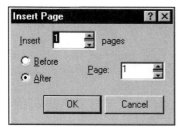

Figure 10. *Enter the number of pages you want to insert and then click OK.*

Click here to add a page before page 1.   Click here to add a page after page 1.

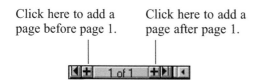

Figure 11. *The Navigator.*

Page flippers

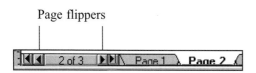

Figure 12. *Use the page flippers to move to the next or previous page.*

To add pages to a document:

1. Select Insert Page from the Layout menu (**Figure 9**) or press the Page Up key on the keyboard. The Insert Page dialog box will appear (**Figure 10**).

2. Enter the number of pages you want to add and whether the new pages should be inserted before or after the specified page, then click OK.

or

1. Look at the bottom left corner of your screen. There you will see several plus signs, and the page you are currently working on (**Figure 11**). This bar is called the *Navigator*.

2. To insert a new page after the current page, click the plus sign to the right of the page counter. Several things will happen:

   ■ A new page will be added.

   ■ One or both of the plus signs will change to arrows (**Figure 12**). These arrows are called *page flippers*.

   ■ Page tabs will appear. You can click any one of the tabs to move to that page.

Tip:

■ The maximum number of pages you can have in one document is 999.

Add Pages to a Document

To delete a page from a document:

1. Select Delete Page from the Layout menu (**Figure 13**). The Delete Page dialog box will open (**Figure 14**), showing the currently selected page. If you want to delete a different page, type that number in the Delete page text box.

2. Click OK.

To delete a range of pages:

1. Open the Delete Page dialog box by selecting Delete Page from the Layout menu.

2. Type the number of the first page you want to delete.

3. Click on the box to the left of Through to page to add a check mark to that box and then type the number of the last page you want to delete (**Figure 15**).

4. Click OK.

Tip:

■ If you remove a page that you did not mean to delete, you can always bring it back by selecting Undo from the Edit menu or by pressing Ctrl+Z on the keyboard.

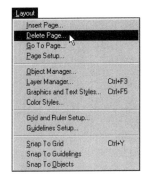

Figure 13. *Select Delete Page from the Layout menu.*

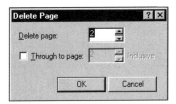

Figure 14. *Type in the page number that you want to delete and then click OK.*

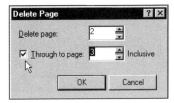

Figure 15. *Check the Through to page box and then enter the last page you want to delete.*

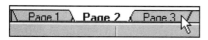

Figure 16. *To move to another page, click the appropriate page tab.*

Click here to move to the first page of the document.   Click here to move to the last page of the document.

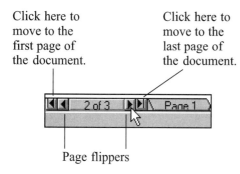

Page flippers

Figure 17. *You can use the page flippers to move to another page.*

Figure 18. *Select Go To Page from the Layout menu.*

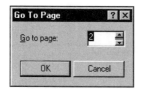

Figure 19. *Use the Go To Page dialog box to move between pages.*

To move between pages:

Click on the appropriate page tab at the bottom left of the screen (**Figure 16**).

or

Click on the right or left pointing arrows—page flippers—that appear on either side of the page counter (**Figure 17**).

or

1. Select Go To Page from the Layout menu (**Figure 18**). The Go To Page dialog box will open (**Figure 19**).

2. Type in the page number you want to move to and click OK.

Tip:

■ The Go To Page dialog box is handy when you are working with a large document. It lets you quickly move from one page to another.

Move Between Pages

I t's important to consider how your drawings are set up on the screen. For instance, when you are working on a complex drawing with many small details, it can be very helpful to view the drawing in two windows. The window on the left would be in a large display size—perhaps 400%—to edit the detail, while the other window would be in a smaller view size so you could see the changes made to the entire drawing.

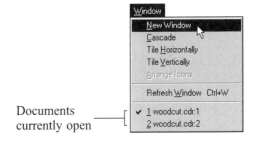

Documents currently open

Figure 20. *Select New Window from the Window menu.*

To view the same drawing in two windows:

1. Open a drawing or get one started in a new document.

2. Select New Window from the Window menu (**Figure 20**). A new window will appear on top of the original (you won't be able to see the first one). If you look up at the title bar, you will notice the graphic's name has a :2 appended to it.

3. Tile the windows by selecting Tile Vertically from the Window menu (**Figure 21**). The two windows will appear side-by-side (**Figure 22**).

Figure 21. *Select Tile Vertically to tile the two windows side-by-side.*

To view two different documents at the same time:

1. Open the two drawings.

2. Select Tile Vertically from the Window menu. The two windows will appear side-by-side.

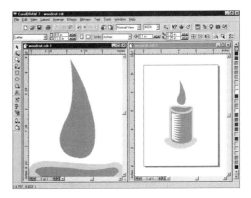

Figure 22. *The same drawing in two windows shown in different display sizes.*

Figure 23. *Open two documents and tile them vertically.*

Figure 24. *Click the Title Bar of the second window to make it active, and then select Paste from the Edit menu. The copied object appears in the second window.*

As you probably know, it's easy to copy files or move files between windows in Windows 95 using drag-and-drop. CorelDraw 7 allows you to do the same thing with your drawings. You can copy an object in one window and paste it into another. In addition, you can move an object from one document to another with a simple drag-and-drop.

To copy an object from one document to another:

1. Open two documents.

2. Tile the documents by selecting Tile Vertically from the Window menu.

3. Use the Pick Tool to select the object you want to copy and select Copy from the Edit menu or press Ctrl+C on the keyboard.

4. Click the Title Bar of the other document's window, the one to which you want to paste the object (**Figure 23**). This will make that window active.

5. Select Paste from the Edit menu or press Ctrl+V on the keyboard. The object will appear in the second document (**Figure 24**).

To move an object from one document to another:

1. Open two documents.

2. Select Tile Vertically from the Window menu to tile the documents.

3. Place the point of the Pick Tool on the outline of the object you want to move. Press the left mouse button and drag it to the other document (**Figure 25**).

4. Release the mouse button when you are happy with the object's new position. The object will move to the other document (**Figure 26**).

Tip:

- You can also move or copy an object from one document to another by dragging the object with the right mouse button. When you release the button, a pop-up menu will appear, asking whether you wish to move or copy the object there.

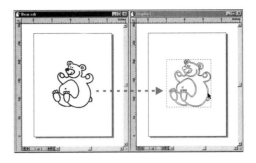

Figure 25. *Use the Pick Tool to drag the object from one document window to another. As you drag the object, a wireframe version of the object appears.*

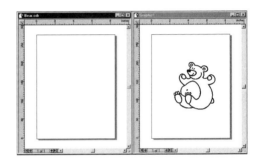

Figure 26. *When you release the mouse button, the object moves to the other document window.*

SUMMARY

In this chapter you learned how to:

- Change page size and orientation
- Change the unit of measure
- Add and delete pages
- Move between pages

- View two documents at once
- Copy an object between documents
- Move an object between two documents

Tools for Precision

CorelDraw 7 includes several tools to help you make your drawings more precise. In this chapter, you will learn how to use the horizontal and vertical rulers, how to change the rulers' *zero point*, and how to change the default unit of measure. Next, you will discover *guidelines*—dashed blue lines that do not print—and find out how they can help you shape and align the objects you draw. From there, you will learn about *grids*—regularly spaced dots that also do not print—and how to effectively use the Status Bar. Finally, you will discover how to *align* your objects by lining them up to a common edge.

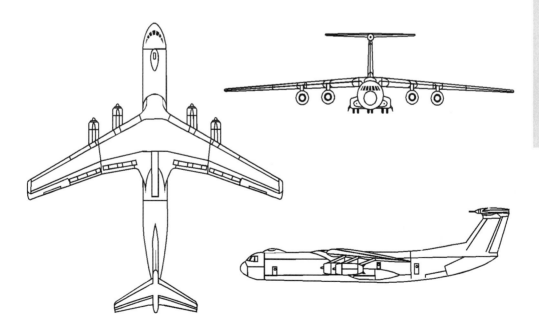

The horizontal ruler is located below the Property Bar and the vertical ruler is on the left side of the screen next to the Toolbox (**Figure 1**). The two rulers meet at a small square on the upper left side of the screen called the *ruler intersection point*. The rulers monitor the location of the mouse using horizontal and vertical *tracking lines*.

All measurements are made from the *zero point*. This is the point where both the vertical and horizontal rulers show a value of 0. By default, the zero point is located at the bottom left corner of the page. This is the standard way the printing industry measures a page. However, you might find it easier to measure a page from the top down.

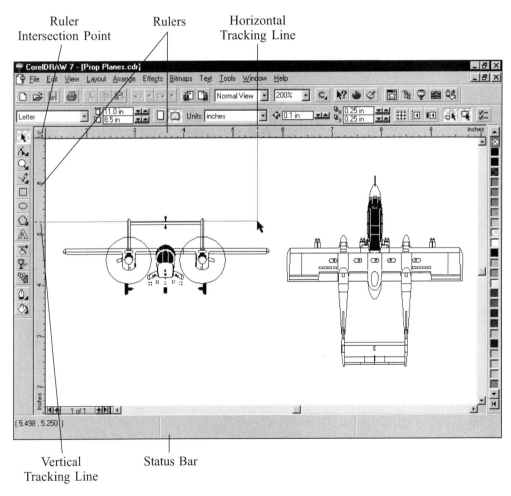

Figure 1. *The rulers, tracking lines, and Status Bar help make your drawings more precise.*

Rulers

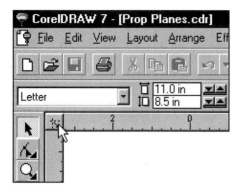

Figure 2. *Place the mouse pointer on the ruler intersection point and then press the left mouse button and drag.*

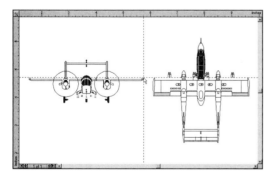

Figure 3. *Drag the dashed lines until they are positioned where you want the new zero point.*

To move the zero point:

1. Move the mouse pointer to the ruler intersection point (**Figure 2**).

2. Press the left mouse button and drag (**Figure 3**). As you do so, two intersecting dashed lines will appear under the mouse cursor.

3. Drag these lines to the position where you would like the zero point to be. For instance, if you want the horizontal and vertical rulers to read 0 at the top left corner of the page, align these dashed lines to the top left corner of the page.

4. When you are happy with the dashed lines' position, release the mouse button. The rulers will redraw and show the new zero point.

Tip:

■ To move the zero point back to the bottom left corner of the page—the default—double-click on the ruler intersection point.

Move the Zero Point

105

To change the rulers' unit of measure for the current document:

1. Select Grid and Ruler Setup from the Layout menu (**Figure 4**) or double-click on either the horizontal or vertical ruler. The Grid & Ruler Setup dialog box will open with the Ruler tab page in front (**Figure 5**).

2. In the Units area of the Ruler tab page, select a new unit of measure from the drop-down list (**Figure 6**).

3. Click OK.

Tip:

■ If the box next to "Same units for Horizontal and Vertical rulers" is not checked, you can select a different measurement unit for each ruler.

Figure 4. *Select Grid and Ruler Setup from the Layout menu.*

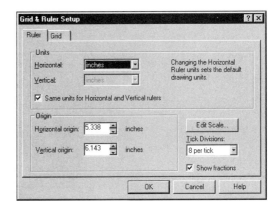

Figure 5. *Use the Grid & Ruler Setup dialog box to set the unit of measure.*

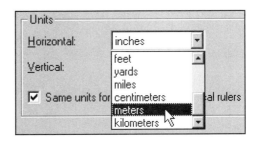

Figure 6. *Click the down arrow next to the Horizontal list box to select a new unit of measure.*

Set a New Unit of Measure

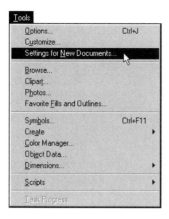

Figure 7. *Select Settings for New Documents from the Tools menu.*

To change the default unit of measure:

1. Open the Grid & Ruler Setup dialog box as described on the previous page and change the measurement unit as desired. Click OK to close the dialog box.

2. Select Settings for New Documents from the Tools menu (**Figure 7**). The Settings for New Documents dialog box will appear (**Figure 8**).

3. Make sure the box next to Grid and rulers is checked, and then click the Save Settings Now button.

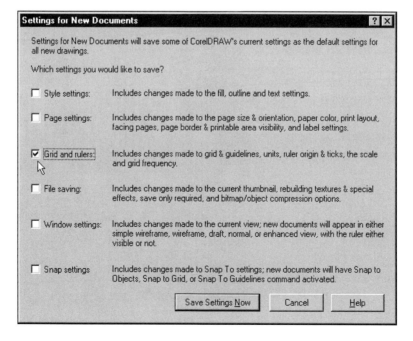

Figure 8. *Make sure the box next to Grid and rulers is checked, and then click Save Settings Now.*

Set the Default Unit of Measure

107

To make the rulers disappear from the screen:

Choose Rulers from the View menu (**Figure 9**). This will remove the check mark that is before Rulers on the View menu and hide the rulers from sight.

Tip:

■ To bring the rulers back again, select Rulers from the View menu.

Figure 9. *Choose Rulers from the View menu.*

I n some cases, you might actually want to bring the ruler right to the area where you are drawing. This can make it easier to watch the vertical and horizontal tracking lines while you draw.

To move a ruler to a new position:

Position the mouse pointer over a ruler, hold down the Shift key, press the left mouse button, and drag the ruler to a new position (**Figure 10**).

Tip:

■ To move a ruler back to its default position near the edge of the screen, hold down the Shift key and double-click on the ruler.

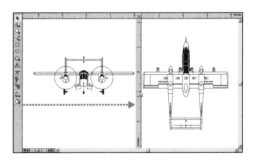

Figure 10. *While pressing the Shift key and the left mouse button, drag the ruler to its new position.*

Guidelines are an extension of rulers that can be positioned anywhere in the drawing window (**Figure 11**). They are very useful for setting up exact areas where you are going to draw and for helping align objects. By default, guidelines do not appear on the printed page, they come in the same flavors as rulers—vertical and horizontal—and can even be angled. A guideline consists of a dashed blue line and two guideline handles—the solid black lines found at each end of the guideline.

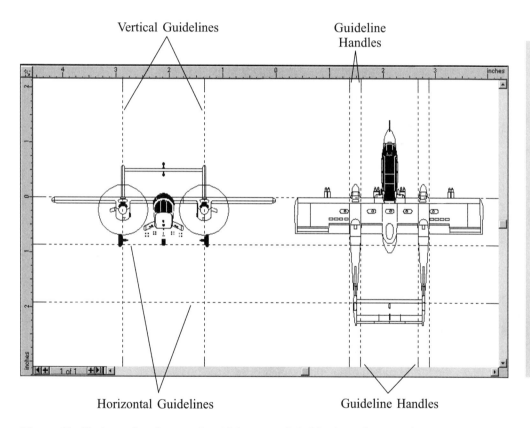

Figure 11. *Horizontal and vertical guidelines are helpful when aligning objects or creating objects of specific sizes.*

To add guidelines to a page:

1. Position the mouse over one of the rulers. Use the horizontal ruler to create horizontal guidelines and vice versa.

2. Press the left mouse button and drag it. A guideline will appear under the mouse pointer (**Figure 12**). Release the mouse button when you are happy with the position of the guideline.

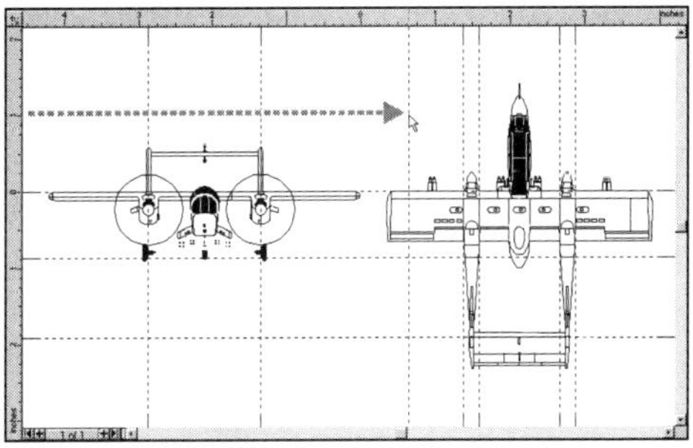

Figure 12. *Position the mouse over a ruler, press the left mouse button, and drag a guideline to the desired position.*

To make a guideline slanted:

1. Position the mouse pointer over a guideline handle. The mouse pointer will change to a double-headed curved arrow.

2. Press the left mouse button and drag the handle until the guideline is at the desired angle (**Figure 13**), and then release the mouse button.

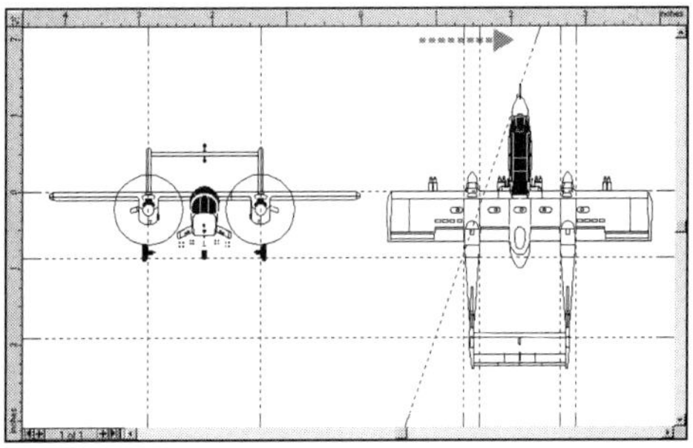

Figure 13. *Drag the guideline handle to angle the guideline.*

To move a guideline:

1. Select the Pick Tool and position the mouse pointer over the guideline.

2. Press the left mouse button and drag the guideline to a new position.

MOVING GUIDELINES

Be careful when you move a guideline—it's easy to accidentally drag an object instead. If this happens, press Ctrl+Z on the keyboard or select Undo from the Edit menu. The object will return right back where it was before you moved it.

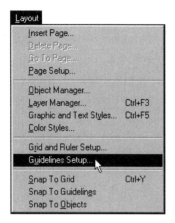

Figure 14. *Select Guidelines Setup from the Layout menu.*

To remove a guideline:

Position the mouse pointer over the guideline, press the left mouse button, and drag the guideline back onto a ruler.

To remove all guidelines:

1. Select Guidelines Setup from the Layout menu (**Figure 14**). The Guidelines Setup dialog box will open (**Figure 15**).

2. Click the Clear All button and then click OK.

Tip:

■ The Guidelines Setup dialog box can be used to add and move guidelines to specific locations. You can also use it to set the exact angle at which a guideline will slant.

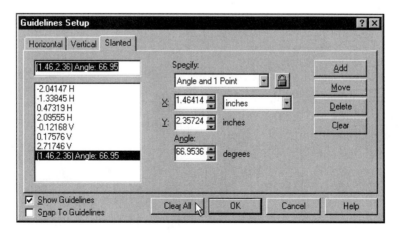

Figure 15. *Click Clear All to remove all guidelines from a document.*

One of the most important guideline features is *Snap to Guidelines* which makes precise alignment easy by forcing an object to line up with a guideline.

To turn on Snap to Guidelines:

1. Add some guidelines to a document.

2. Choose Snap To Guidelines from the Layout menu (**Figure 16**).

3. Test the Snap to Guidelines feature by selecting the Rectangle Tool and drawing a rectangle near the guidelines. As you draw, the rectangle's edges will "snap to" the guideline.

Tip:

- A check mark will appear in front of the Snap To Guidelines item on the Layout menu when this feature is turned on.

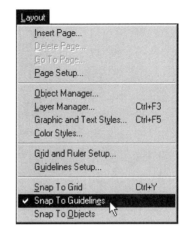

Figure 16. *Choose Snap To Guidelines from the Layout menu.*

Grids are extremely useful for creating precision drawings such as flowcharts, office layout plans, blueprints for buildings, and anything that requires straight lines, uniform shapes, and perfect alignment. The grid dots that appear on the screen when you setup a grid do not print (**Figure 17**).

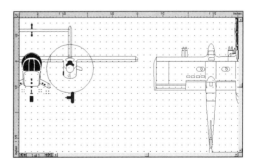

Figure 17. *Grid dots do not print and are helpful when aligning objects.*

Snap To Guidelines; Grids

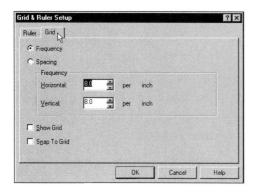

Figure 18. *Click the Grid tab to bring that page to the front.*

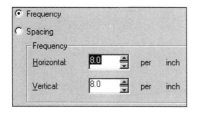

Figure 19. *You can create a grid by setting how many grid dots will appear per measurement unit.*

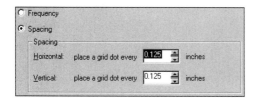

Figure 20. *Or you can create a grid by setting how far apart each grid dot will be.*

To setup a grid:

1. Select Grid and Ruler Setup from the Layout menu or double-click on a ruler. The Grid & Ruler Setup dialog box will open with the Ruler tab page in front.

2. Click on the Grid tab to bring that page to the front (**Figure 18**).

3. You can set how many grid dots appear on the screen in two ways:

   - By Frequency: click the option button next to Frequency, then use the Frequency area (**Figure 19**) to type in how many dots will appear per the default unit of measure. In Figure 19, the grid will contain 8 dots per inch (1 dot every 1/8 inch).

   - By Spacing: click the option button next to Spacing, then use the Spacing area (**Figure 20**) to set the placement of each grid dot. In Figure 20, the grid will place 1 dot every .125 inch (1/8 inch).

4. Check the box next to Show Grid.

5. Check the box next to Snap To Grid. This feature works just like Snap to Guidelines described on the previous page. Any object you create will automatically "snap to" a grid dot.

6. Click OK. The grid will appear on the screen (**Figure 17**).

7. Test out the grid by selecting a drawing tool and creating an object.

Setup a Grid

The Status Bar (**Figure 21**) gives you information about everything you do in CorelDraw—the position of the mouse, what Snap To constraints are on, what kind of object is selected and its details, including size, position, and color. You can tailor the Status Bar to provide the information you need.

By default the Status Bar is one line width high. This saves valuable screen real estate, but does hide information. If you need to see more information about an object, you will need to make the Status Bar bigger.

Figure 21. *The Status Bar gives you detailed information about your graphics.*

To make the Status Bar bigger:

1. Right mouse click on the Status Bar. A pop-up menu will appear (**Figure 22**).

2. Click Large Status Bar.

or

Position the mouse pointer over the upper edge of the Status Bar, press the left mouse button, and drag it upward.

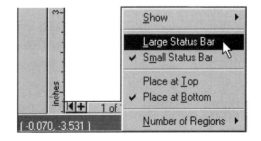

Figure 22. *Click Large Status Bar on the pop-up menu.*

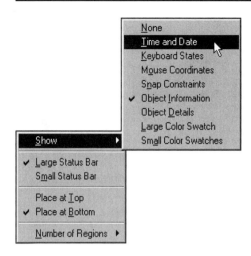

Figure 23. *Right mouse click on the Status Bar to display the pop-up menu. Click the Show item to make the fly-out menu open.*

Figure 24. *Point the mouse at one of the vertical separators, press the mouse button, and drag it to a new position.*

To change the Status Bar information:

1. Right mouse click on the Status Bar. A pop-up menu will appear.

2. Click on the Show item to display the fly-out (**Figure 23**). You can view many things, including:

   ■ Time and Date

   ■ Keyboard States—whether Caps Lock, Num Lock, Scroll Lock, or Overwrite are on

   ■ Mouse Coordinates

   ■ Snap Constraints—which Snap To features are on

   ■ Small or Large Swatches— these show an object's outline width and color, and the object's fill color.

3. Choose the information that you want to view from the pop-up menu.

The Status Bar is divided into three *regions*. Sometimes the information displayed in one of these regions is wider than the region is. You can make a region larger by moving one of the *vertical separators*.

To make a region larger:

1. Position the mouse pointer over a vertical separator. The pointer will change to a double-headed arrow (**Figure 24**).

2. Press the left mouse button and drag the separator to a new position.

Change Information on the Status Bar

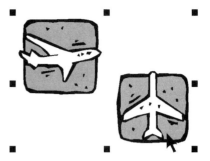

Figure 25. *Use the Pick Tool to select two or more objects to be aligned.*

Every object has handles that surround the object when it is selected with the Pick Tool. These handles also serve another purpose—they make up an invisible rectangular boundary around objects. In other words, they are there, working, even if you can't see them. This boundary is used when *aligning* objects. When objects are aligned, they are lined up using a common boundary edge. For instance if two objects are aligned to the left, this means the objects are lined up using the invisible left boundary of each object.

To align objects:

1. Select two or more objects using the Pick Tool (**Figure 25**).

2. Choose Align and Distribute from the Arrange menu (**Figure 26**), press Ctrl+A on the keyboard, or click the Align button on the Property Bar. This will open the Align and Distribute dialog box with the Align tab page in front (**Figure 27**).

3. Select the type of alignment that you want—vertical and/or horizontal. You can align objects in two dimensions (horizontally and vertically) at the same time, or just in one dimension.

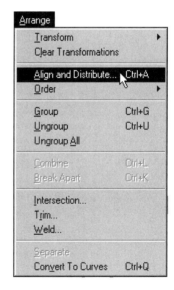

Figure 26. *Select Align and Distribute from the Arrange menu or press Ctrl+A on the keyboard.*

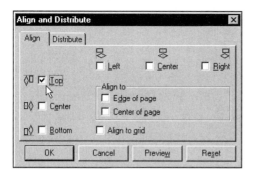

Figure 27. *Put checks in the check boxes next to the type of alignment you want.*

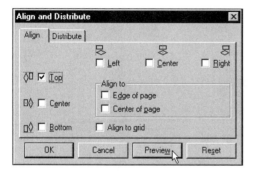

Figure 28. *Click the Preview button to see the objects you selected align in the drawing window. If you like the alignment, click OK, otherwise click Reset and try a different type of alignment. The two jets in this figure have been aligned to the Top (compare them with Figure 25).*

4. Click the Preview button to see the results of what you have chosen without committing yourself (**Figure 28**). If you like what you see, click OK. If you want to select another type of alignment, click Reset. The objects will move back to their original positions and you can try again.

Tips:

- If you select objects by holding down the shift key and clicking on them—*multiple selecting*—the last object you select will be the target object that CorelDraw will use. For instance, if you use multiple selection and align the objects' right edges, the objects will align to the right edge of the last object you selected.

- If you marquee select the objects, the lowest object on the page is the one that CorelDraw 7 will use as the target to align the other objects.

Align Objects

TYPES OF ALIGNMENT

The Align tab page of the Align and Distribute dialog box shows small pictures by the horizontal and vertical alignment check boxes to give you a hint as to what the alignment will do. These little pictures can be confusing, so below are illustrations that show how the vertical and horizontal alignment works together. In the caption below each illustration, the first word is the vertical alignment and the second word is the horizontal alignment.

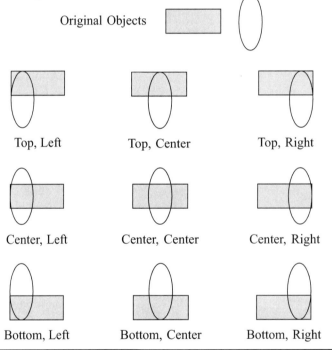

Original Objects

Top, Left　　　Top, Center　　　Top, Right

Center, Left　　　Center, Center　　　Center, Right

Bottom, Left　　　Bottom, Center　　　Bottom, Right

SUMMARY

In this chapter you learned how to:

- Set the zero point
- Change the unit of measure
- Move the rulers
- Add, move, and delete guidelines

- Create slanted guidelines
- Setup a grid
- Use the snap to features
- Set Status Bar information
- Align objects

Color and Fills

I

n this chapter, you will learn how to *fill* closed objects with *uniform*, *fountain*, *pattern*, and *texture* fills, and change the outline color of objects. The tools you will use to do these things are the Color Palette, the Fill Tool and its fly-out, and a new CorelDraw 7 tool, the Interactive Fill Tool (**Figure 1**).

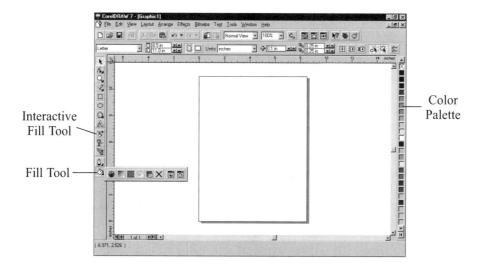

Interactive Fill Tool

Fill Tool

Color Palette

Figure 1. *The Fill Tool, Interactive Fill Tool, and Color Palette will make your drawings colorful.*

Types of Fills; Tools You Will Use

olor can bring a drawing to life and adding a solid color fill—called a *uniform fill*—to an object is very easy. But, before an object can be filled with color, the object has to have a closed path.

Figure 2. *Press the Auto-Close button on the Property Bar to close the object's path.*

To make sure an object has a closed path:

1. Select the object with the Pick Tool and look up at the right side of the Property Bar. If the Auto-Close button is available (**Figure 2**), then the curve is open; if not, then the curve is closed.

2. To close the curve, press the Auto-Close button.

Figure 3. *Select the closed objects with the Pick Tool.*

To fill objects with a uniform color:

1. Select one or more closed objects with the Pick Tool (**Figure 3**).

2. Click on one of the *color wells* on the Color Palette located at the right side of the screen (**Figure 4**). The objects will fill with that color (**Figure 5**).

Figure 4. *Click on a color well to fill the objects with that color.*

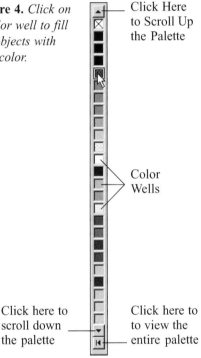

Click Here to Scroll Up the Palette

Color Wells

Click here to scroll down the palette

Click here to to view the entire palette

Tip:

- To see more available colors on the Color Palette, use the up and down arrows at the top and bottom of the palette.

- To view the entire Color Palette, click the button at the bottom of the palette.

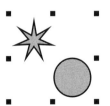

Figure 5. *When you click on a color well, the selected objects fill with that color.*

Close an Object's Path; Fill with Color

Figure 6. *Left or right mouse click the color well with an X in it to remove any color fills or outlines from objects.*

WHERE'S THE COLOR PALETTE?

If you don't see the Color Palette, you can open it by selecting Custom Colors from the Color Palette fly-out on the View menu.

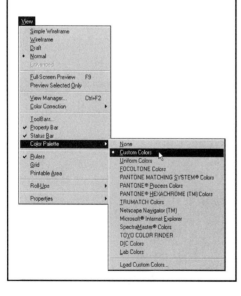

To change the outline color of objects:

1. Use the Pick Tool to select the objects you want to change.

2. Right mouse click on one of the color wells on the Color Palette. The objects' outlines will change to that color.

To remove color from objects:

1. Select the objects using the Pick Tool.

2. To remove the fill, left mouse click on the color well at the top of the Color Palette that has an X in it (**Figure 6**). To remove the objects' outline color, right mouse click on that same color well.

Tip:

■ Be careful when removing both the fill and outline color of an object. If the object is not selected, you won't be able to see it and may lose track of it!

Change Outline Color; Remove Color

By default, the Color Palette shows a custom set of colors. However, there are many color sets and *color matching systems* to choose from. CorelDraw 7 includes 12 color sets and matching systems that are available for display in the Color Palette. (To find out about color matching systems, see the sidebar on the next page.)

To display a different color set in the Color Palette:

1. Select Color Palette from the View menu (**Figure 7**). This will open the Color Palette fly-out.

2. Click the color set you want to display.

Tip:

■ You can also view the Color Palette fly-out by clicking the right mouse button on an unused place on the page and selecting View from the pop-up menu, then selecting Color Palette on the fly-out.

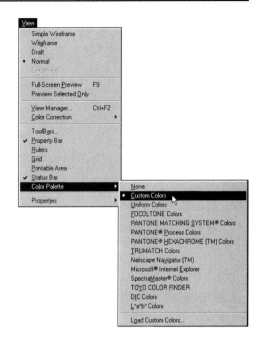

Figure 7. *Select Color Palette from the View menu to display the color sets available on the fly-out.*

WORLD WIDE WEB COLOR PALETTES

CorelDraw 7 includes two new palettes, one for Microsoft Internet Explorer, and another for Netscape Navigator. These palettes include the 256 colors that these Internet browsers correctly display. For more information about graphics and the World Wide Web, check out Chapter 17, *Creating Graphics for the Web*.

WHAT IS A COLOR MATCHING SYSTEM?

Color matching systems are used by designers to tell commercial printers exactly what color to use for a print job. A matching system assigns numbers to different colors and displays them in *swatch books* that can be bought at art supply stores. Suppose that you want to use "fire engine red" for the title of a brochure. You would look through a color swatch book to find the exact red you have in mind, then tell the printer what that color number is. A few color matching systems are Pantone, Spectramaster, Toyo, and Trumatch.

WHAT IS A COLOR MODEL?

A color model breaks colors down into base or primary colors. If you are familiar with a color wheel, you know that red, yellow, and blue are the primary colors that can be used to make up all the colors our eyes can see. Printers use a different group of primary colors: cyan, magenta, yellow, and black. These four colors make up the *CMYK* color model (black is represented by the letter K because printers refer to this as the *key color*). Other color models include HSB (hue, saturation, and brightness) and RGB (red, green, blue).

SPOT COLOR AND PROCESS COLOR

If you work with a commercial printer, you will probably hear the terms *spot color* and *process color*. Spot color refers to a color matching system such as Pantone, and process color refers to a color model such as CMYK. The conceptual difference is that a color matching system is based on a recipe of specific mixed inks, whereas process color is based on the proportionate break down of real-world colors into each of the primary colors that they contain.

About Colors

To create custom colors:

1. Select the object you want to fill with the custom color.

2. Click the Fill Tool to display the fly-out, then click the Fill Color button (**Figure 8**). This will open the Uniform Fill dialog box (**Figure 9**).

3. Use the palette at the bottom of the dialog box to find the closest color to the one you want to create. When you have found that color, click on it (**Figure 10**).

4. Move the squares on the color cube to the right of the dialog box to change the primary color values (**Figure 11**). To darken the color, slide the bar to the right of the cube upwards. This will add black.

5. Type a name into the text box next to Name (this is optional).

6. Click OK. The item you selected will be filled with the new color, and the color will be added to the bottom of the Color Palette.

Figure 8. *Click the Fill Tool to display the fly-out, then click the Fill Color button.*

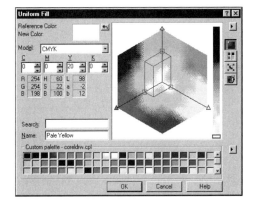

Figure 9. *Use the Uniform Fill dialog box to create custom colors.*

Figure 10. *Select a color from the custom palette that is closest to the one you want to create.*

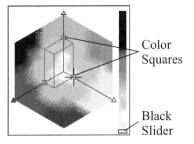

Color Squares

Black Slider

Figure 11. *Drag the squares on the color cube to create your custom color.*

Create Custom Colors

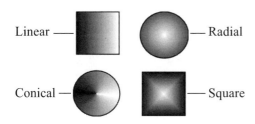

Figure 12. *There are four types of fountain fills.*

Figure 13. *The Interactive Fill Tool.*

Figure 14. *Click and drag the Interactive Fill Tool to fill an object with a linear fountain fill.*

Figure 15. *When you release the mouse, the object redraws with the new fill.*

A fountain fill is a gradual blend between two or more colors across a closed path object. There are four types of fountain fills (**Figure 12**):

- linear—the blend of colors moves in a straight line
- radial—the blend of colors moves in concentric circles from the center
- conical—the blend of colors moves in a circular path, radiating from the center
- square—the blend of colors moves in a series of concentric squares that radiate from the center

A dding special fills is easy now that CorelDraw 7 includes the Interactive Fill Tool (**Figure 13**). All you have to do is click and drag to add the fill.

To add a linear fountain fill to an object:

1. Make sure the object is made up of a closed path.

2. Select the Interactive Fill Tool. A little paint bucket will appear under the mouse pointer.

3. Click the object to select it.

4. Position the mouse on the side of the object where you want the fill to begin, then press the left mouse button and drag it to the other side of the object where you want the fill to end (**Figure 14**).

5. Release the mouse. The object will redraw with a fountain fill (**Figure 15**).

Fountain Fills; Add a Linear Fountain Fill

To change the type of fountain fill:

1. Fill the closed path object with a Linear Fountain Fill.

2. Select the type of Fountain Fill that you want—linear, radial, conical, or square—by clicking the appropriate button on the Property Bar (**Figure 16**). The object will redraw with that fill.

To change the fountain fill colors of an object:

1. Select the Interactive Fill Tool, then click the fountain-filled object to select it.

2. Use the Fill Color drop-down lists on the Property Bar to select new start and end colors (**Figure 17**).

or

1. Select the object using the Pick Tool.

2. Click the Fill Tool to view the fly-out, then click the Special Fill Roll-Up button (**Figure 18**). That roll-up will appear (**Figure 19**).

3. Use the drop-down color lists to select new start and end colors.

4. Click Apply.

Tip:

■ The changes you make will only apply to the selected object.

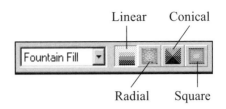

Figure 16. *To change the type of fountain fill, click the appropriate button on the Property Bar.*

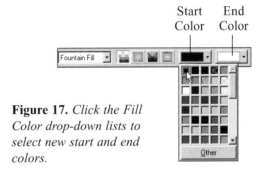

Figure 17. *Click the Fill Color drop-down lists to select new start and end colors.*

Figure 18. *Click the Special Fill Roll-Up button on the Fill Tool fly-out.*

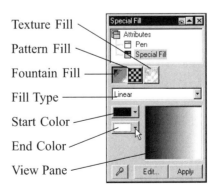

Figure 19. *Use the Special Fill Roll-Up to select new start and end colors.*

Figure 20. *Add a fountain fill to a closed path object using the Interactive Fill Tool.*

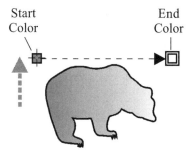

Start Color · · · · · End Color

Figure 21. *Press and drag the mouse to move the start color square to its new position. As you drag the start color square, the end color square will follow along.*

Figure 22. *Move the end color square to its new position.*

To move the start color and end color positions:

1. Add a fountain fill to an object using the Interactive Fill Tool (**Figure 20**).

2. Position the Interactive Fill Tool over the start color square. The mouse will change to a cross-hair.

3. Press the left mouse button and drag the color square to the desired position (**Figure 21**), then release the mouse button.

4. Position the mouse over the end color square. Press the left mouse button and drag this square to its new position (**Figure 22**).

Tip:

- You can place the start and end color squares anywhere inside or outside the object. For instance, you could move the start color to the edge of an object and move the end color to the middle.

Move the Start Color and End Color Positions

To add intermediate colors to a fountain fill:

1. Add a fountain fill to an object using the Interactive Fill Tool (**Figure 23**).

2. Find the color on the Color Palette that you want to add between the start and end colors of the Fountain Fill.

3. Position the mouse over that color, press the left mouse button, and drag that color square onto the dashed line between the start and end color squares. As you drag the color from the palette, the mouse pointer will have a slash circle attached to it (**Figure 24**). You'll know you are in the right place when the mouse pointer changes to a pointer with a little plus sign attached to it (**Figure 25**).

4. Release the mouse. The color will be added to the fountain fill.

Tip:

■ You can add as many intermediate colors as you want.

Figure 23. *Add a fountain fill to an object.*

Figure 24. *Drag the intermediate color from the Color Palette using the Interactive Fill Tool.*

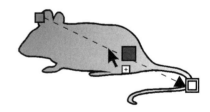

Figure 25. *Release the mouse button when the pointer changes from a slash circle to a plus sign.*

Figure 26. *Select Pattern Fill from the Fill Type drop-down list.*

Figure 27. *When you select Pattern Fill, the selected object will be filled with the default pattern.*

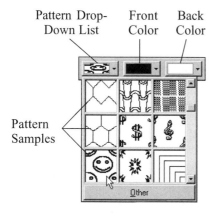

Figure 28. *Click on a pattern sample to select that pattern.*

Figure 29. *The selected object will fill with the new pattern.*

Patterns are fun and can add interesting effects to your graphics. There are three types of pattern fills you can select: Two Color, Full Color, and Bitmap.

To add a two-color pattern fill to an object:

1. Make sure the object has a closed path, then select it with the Interactive Fill Tool.

2. Select Pattern Fill from the Fill Type drop-down list on the Property Bar (**Figure 26**). Your object will be filled with the default, a two-color pattern, large black dots on a white background (**Figure 27**).

3. To change the pattern, click the Pattern drop-down list on the Property Bar (**Figure 28**) and select another pattern. The graphic will be filled with that new pattern (**Figure 29**).

Tips:

- To change the color of the pattern, use the Front Color and Back Color drop-down lists next to the Pattern drop-down list on the Property Bar.

- You can create your own patterns, by clicking the Other button at the bottom of the Pattern drop-down list (**Figure 28**) and then using the Two-Color Pattern Editor that opens.

Add a Two Color Pattern Fill to an Object

To add a full color or bitmap pattern fill to an object:

1. Make sure the object has a closed path, then select it with the Interactive Fill Tool.

2. Use the drop-down list to choose Pattern Fill on the Property Bar, and click the Full Colors Pattern Fill button or the Bitmap Pattern button on the Property Bar (**Figure 30**).

3. Use the Pattern drop-down list to select a pattern (**Figure 31**). Your graphic will redraw, filled with that pattern (**Figure 32**).

Tip:

- To make the pattern smaller or larger, click the Small (Sm), Medium (Md), or Large (Lg) buttons on the Property Bar.

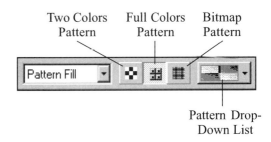

Figure 30. *Click either the Full Colors Pattern Fill button or the Bitmap Pattern Fill button.*

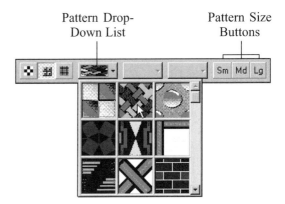

Figure 31. *Click on a pattern from the drop-down list.*

Figure 32. *The object will fill with the new pattern.*

Add Full Color or Bitmap Pattern Fills

Figure 33. *Select a closed path object with the Interactive Fill Tool.*

Fill Type Drop-   Texture   Texture Drop-
Down List   Libraries   Down List

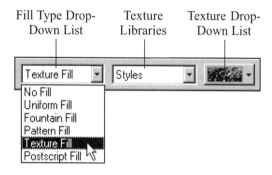

Figure 34. *Select Texture Fill from the Fill Type drop-down list.*

Figure 35. *Click on a texture from the drop-down list.*

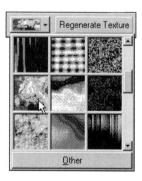

Textures create interesting effects, and you can easily add them to your drawings. CorelDraw 7 comes with hundreds of preset textures that you can modify to suit your needs.

To add a texture fill to an object:

1. Make sure the object has a closed path and select it with the Interactive Fill Tool (**Figure 33**).

2. Select Texture Fill from the Fill Type drop-down list on the Property Bar (**Figure 34**).

3. Use the Texture drop-down list to find a fill (**Figure 35**). Click on the fill of your choice. Your object will redraw with that texture (**Figure 36**).

Tip:

■ CorelDraw 7 comes with hundreds of textures stored in different libaries. To view the different libraries, use the Texture Libraries drop-down list on the Property Bar (**Figure 34**) to select a library, and then click the Texture drop-down list button to view the textures.

Figure 36. *The selected object redraws, filled with the new texture.*

Add a Texture to an Object

To customize a texture:

1. Fill a closed path object with a texture fill as described on the previous page, but when you go to select a texture from the Texture drop-down list, click the Other button (**Figure 37**). The Texture Fill dialog box will open (**Figure 38**).

2. Use this dialog box, to select a texture from the Texture list and customize the texture's colors using the buttons on the lower right side of the dialog box. To see the texture you have created, click the Preview button. The customized texture will appear in the preview pane. If you are happy with the texture, click OK. Your object will redraw with the new texture fill.

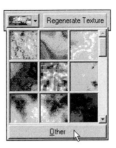

Figure 37. *Click the Other button on the Texture drop-down list.*

Texture Libraries   Texture List   Preview Pane

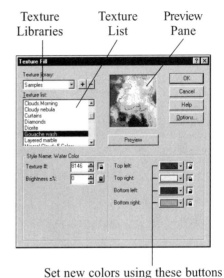

Set new colors using these buttons

Figure 38. *You can create custom textures using the Texture Fill dialog box.*

Create a Custom Texture

SUMMARY:

In this chapter you learned how to:

- Add uniform fills to objects
- Change objects' outline color
- Add fountain fills to objects
- Change the fountain fill colors
- Add intermediate colors to a fountain fill
- Add pattern fills to objects
- Add texture fills to objects
- Customize texture fills

Working with Text   *11*

$\mathcal{P}$ictures can be worth a thousand words, but sometimes you also need words to convey your message to the world. For instance, it's hard to imagine brochures, pamphlets, or postcards without some text.

Text comes in two flavors in CorelDraw 7. *Artistic text* is used for single text lines such as titles or for text to which you want to add a special effect, such as *fitting text to a path. Paragraph text* is used for text-intensive projects such as brochures, ads, or newsletters. Any text created in CorelDraw 7, whether it's artistic or paragraph, makes up a *text object*.

In this chapter, you will learn how to add artistic and paragraph text, change fonts, change spacing between characters and lines, and convert artistic text to paragraph text and back again. From there, you will import text into a document, make it flow between text frames, add bullets to a list, and quickly create drop caps.

Artistic and Paragraph Text

CorelDraw Ships with Over 1400 Fonts

Included on CorelDraw CD-ROM disk 1 are more than 1400 typefaces you can load onto your computer system. To view the fonts individually, so you can decide which ones you want to load on your system, use the Corel Multimedia Manager that ships with CorelDraw 7. To load new fonts on your system, use the Font application found in the Windows 95 Control Panel. The fonts are located alphabetically under the Font folder on the CD-ROM. A word of warning, though. Windows 95 can only handle about 500 fonts on a system at one time. If you load this many fonts on your computer, the time it takes Windows 95 to boot up will become quite long.

To add artistic text:

Figure 1. *The Text Tool.*

1. Select the Text Tool (**Figure 1**) or press F8 on the keyboard. The mouse pointer will change to a cross-hair with a tiny "A" attached to it.

2. Click on the place where you wish the artistic text to start. A vertical line will appear where you clicked. This is called the *insertion marker*.

3. Type your text. As you type, the corresponding characters will appear on the screen (**Figure 2**).

4. When you are finished typing, select the Pick Tool. Eight black handles will appear around the text object, showing that it is selected (**Figure 3**).

Figure 2. *As you type, the corresponding characters appear on the screen.*

Figure 3. *When you finish typing and select the Pick Tool, eight handles appear around the text object.*

WHAT ARE THOSE SQUIGGLY RED LINES UNDER MY WORDS?

As you type, CorelDraw 7 checks your spelling. If there are any squiggly red lines underneath a word after you have finished typing, this means that the word could be spelled incorrectly (or is not in the program's dictionary). To check spellings that CorelDraw 7's dictionary suggests, select the Text Tool, then right mouse click on the word. A pop-up menu with spelling suggestions will appear (**Figure 4**). Click the correctly spelled word to replace the misspelled one in the text object.

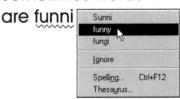

Figure 4. *Use the Text Tool to right mouse click on the word, then select a suggested word from the pop-up menu.*

Add Artistic Text

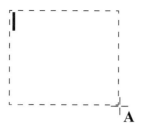

Figure 5. *Press the left mouse button and drag the Text Tool to create a marquee.*

Figure 6. *As you type, the corresponding characters appear in the dashed frame. (A. A. Milne wrote this sentence.)*

Text Handle

Text Handle

Figure 7. *When paragraph text is selected there are six black handles and two text handles around the text frame.*

To add paragraph text:

1. Select the Text Tool.

2. Position the mouse cross-hair on the place where you would like the text to start.

3. Press the left mouse button and drag it diagonally. As you drag a dashed rectangle will appear (**Figure 5**). When you release the mouse button, an insertion marker will appear at the upper left of the marquee.

4. Type your text. As you type, the corresponding characters will appear in the dashed frame (**Figure 6**).

5. When you are finished, select the Pick Tool. The dashed rectangle will change to a paragraph text frame (**Figure 7**). Six black handles will appear to the right and left of the frame and two *text handles* will also appear—one at the top and one at the bottom.

FONTS USED IN THIS BOOK

The drop caps used in each chapter of this book are all available on CorelDraw CD-ROM disk 1. If you see a font you like, look in Appendix A for the font name.

Add Paragraph Text

To convert artistic text to paragraph text:

1. Select the artistic text object with the Pick Tool (**Figure 8**).

2. Choose Convert to Paragraph Text from the Text menu (**Figure 9**). A paragraph text frame will appear around the text (**Figure 10**).

To convert paragraph text to artistic text:

1. Select the paragraph text object with the Pick Tool.

2. Choose Convert to Artistic Text from the Text menu (**Figure 11**).

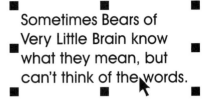

Figure 8. *Select the artistic text object with the Pick Tool.*

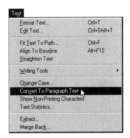

Figure 9. *Choose Convert to Paragraph Text from the Text menu.*

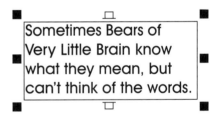

Figure 10. *A paragraph text frame appears around the text.*

Figure 11. *Choose Convert to Artistic Text from the Text menu.*

WATCH THE STATUS BAR

When a text object is selected the Status Bar will always tell you whether it's artistic or paragraph text and what font and font size are being used.

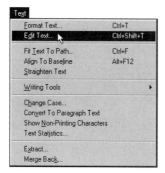

Figure 12. *Select Edit Text from the Text menu or press Ctrl+Shift+T on the keyboard.*

Figure 13. *Use the Edit Text dialog box to edit your text.*

To edit artistic or paragraph text:

1. Select the text object with the Pick Tool.

2. Choose Edit Text from the Text menu (**Figure 12**) or press Ctrl+Shift+T on the keyboard. The Edit Text dialog will appear (**Figure 13**).

3. Edit the text in the window, then click OK.

or

1. Select the Text Tool, then position the mouse over the text to be edited.

2. Click the left mouse button. The insertion marker will appear there.

3. Edit the text.

Tips:

- The second text editing method should only be used for editing small amounts of text. If you need to edit a large section of text, use the Edit Text dialog box.

- You must use the Edit Text dialog box to edit artistic text that has had any of the following special effects applied to it: Perspective, Envelope, or Extrude. (To check out these special effects, take a look at Chapter 15, *Special Effects*.)

Edit Text

When you add text, CorelDraw 7 uses a default font (AvantGarde), font size (24 points), justification (none), and character and line spacing (100% of character size). To change these attributes, you will need to *format* the text using the Format Text dialog box.

To change the font of a text object:

1. Select the text object with the Pick Tool (**Figure 14**).

2. Choose Format Text from the Text menu (**Figure 15**) or press Ctrl+T on the keyboard. The Format Text dialog box will open with the Font tab page in front (**Figure 16**).

3. Click on a font name in the Font List Box to select it. A preview of that font will appear in the preview pane.

4. Click OK. The text will redraw in the new font (**Figure 17**).

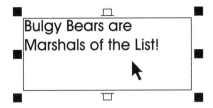

Figure 14. *Select the text object with the Pick Tool.*

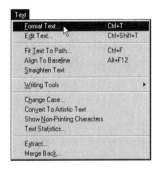

Figure 15. *Choose Format Text from the Text menu or press Ctrl+T on the keyboard.*

Selected Font   Font List   Preview Pane

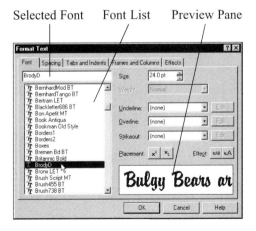

Figure 16. *Click a font name in the Font List to see a sample of it in the view pane.*

Figure 17. *After you click OK, the text redraws using the newly selected font.*

Change Fonts

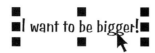

Figure 18. *Select the text object you want to change with the Pick Tool.*

Figure 19. *Use the Size text box found in the Format Text dialog box to enter a new font size.*

Figure 20. *After you click OK, the text redraws in the new size.*

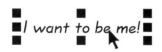

Figure 21. *Select the text object with the Pick Tool.*

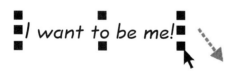

Figure 22a. *Stretching text proportionally.*

Figure 22b. *Stretching text horizontally.*

To change the size of paragraph or artistic text characters:

1. Select the text object with the Pick Tool (**Figure 18**).

2. Open the Format Text dialog box by pressing Ctrl+T on the keyboard or choosing Format Text from the Text menu (**Figure 16**).

3. Type a number in the Size text box (**Figure 19**). The default unit for type is points.

4. Click OK. Your text will redraw with that point size (**Figure 20**).

Another way to change artistic or paragraph text character size:

1. Select the artistic text object with the Pick Tool (**Figure 21**). This will display the eight black handles that surround the text object.

2. If you are resizing artistic text, drag the appropriate handle to stretch the text proportionally, horizontally, or vertically (**Figures 22a–c**). If you are resizing paragraph text, hold down the Alt key and drag a corner handle.

Figure 22c. *Stretching text vertically.*

Change Font Size

To change the formatting of individual characters:

1. Zoom in on the text object using the Zoom Tool.

2. Select the Text Tool, then position the mouse to the left of the character you want to change (**Figure 23**).

3. Press the left mouse button and drag it to the right to select the character (**Figure 24**).

4. Open the Format Text dialog box by selecting Format Text from the Text menu or pressing Ctrl+T on the keyboard. Change the character's attributes—font and/or font size—then click OK. The letter will redraw with the changes you have made (**Figure 25**).

Tip:

- You can change the formatting of several letters at once by dragging the mouse to select several letters.

Change Ime!

Figure 23. *Position the insertion marker before the character you want to change.*

Change me!

Figure 24. *Press the left mouse button and drag the insertion marker until the letter is selected.*

Change 𝑚e!

Figure 25. *After you click OK, the letter redraws with the new formatting.*

Format Individual Characters

WHAT KIND OF JUSTIFICATION DO YOU WANT?

There are five ways you can justify a text block in CorelDraw 7. Below is a sample of each type.

I am left justified.	I am center justified.	I am right justified.	I am full justified.	I am f o r c e justified.

Figure 26. *Select the text object with the Pick Tool.*

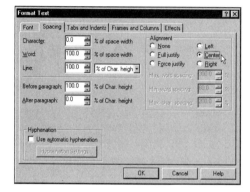

Figure 27. *Use the Spacing tab page of the Format Text dialog box to change the text's justification.*

Figure 28. *When you click OK, the text redraws with the new centered justification.*

To change the text object's justification:

1. Select the text object with the Pick Tool (**Figure 26**).

2. Choose Format Text from the Text menu or press Ctrl+T on the keyboard. The Format Text dialog box will open with the Font tab page in front.

3. Click on the Spacing tab to bring that page to the front (**Figure 27**).

4. On the upper-right side of the Spacing tab page, use the Alignment area to select the type of justification.

5. Click OK. Your text will change to assume that type of justification (**Figure 28**).

> ### THE FORMAT TEXT DIALOG BOX IS CONTEXT SENSITIVE
>
> If you compare Figure 27 with Figure 32, you will notice that the Spacing tab page is different. The reason for this is that the Format Text dialog box is context sensitive. It displays different options depending upon the selected text object. In Figure 27, a paragraph text object is selected, whereas in Figure 32, an artistic text object is selected.

Change Justification

Figure 29. *Select the text object with the Shape Tool.*

The space between characters is called *kerning* and the distance from the bottom of one line of text to the bottom of the next is called *leading*. These are terms that desktop publishers use all the time. There are several ways to change kerning and leading in CorelDraw 7.

To let CorelDraw kern the space equally between all characters:

1. Create the text object.

2. Select the Shape Tool, then use it to click on the text object (**Figure 29**). This will select the text object and two arrows will appear connected to the object—one on the lower left pointing downward, and one on the lower right pointing to the right.

Figure 30. *Drag the lower right arrow to the right to add more space between characters.*

3. Position the Shape Tool over the arrow on the lower right corner.

4. Press the left mouse button and drag the mouse to the right to add space between the letters (**Figure 30**) or drag the mouse to the left to decrease the amount of space between the letters (**Figure 31**).

or

1. Create the text object.

2. Select it using the Pick Tool, then open the Format Text dialog box by pressing Ctrl+T on the keyboard or selecting Format Text from the Text menu.

3. Click on the Spacing tab to move to that tab page (**Figure 32**).

Figure 31. *Drag the lower right arrow to the left to decrease the space between characters.*

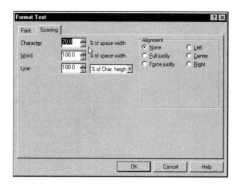

Figure 32. *Use the Spacing tab page of the Format Text dialog box to set the amount of space between characters.*

Figure 33. *Select the text object with the Shape Tool. A node will appear at the lower left of each character.*

Figure 34. *Position the Shape Tool over the node that corresponds to the character you want to move, then press the left mouse button and drag the character to its new position.*

4. Use the text box next to Character in the upper left corner to set the percentage of space width (this is based on the size of the font).

5. Click OK.

Tip:

■ You can also set the amount of space between words using the Format Text dialog box. To change the inter-word spacing, type a number into the Word text box (it is located directly under the Character text box) on the Spacing tab.

To kern individual characters:

1. Use the Zoom Tool to zoom in on the text object.

2. Select the text object with the Shape Tool. A node will appear at the lower left of each character (**Figure 33**).

3. Position the mouse pointer over the node that corresponds to the character you want to move.

4. Press the left mouse button and drag that character to its new position (**Figure 34**). As you drag, a blue dashed version of the character will appear.

Tip:

■ If you want to move several letters at once, you can select several nodes by holding down the Shift key while clicking on each node or pressing the left mouse button and dragging a marquee around the desired nodes.

Manual Kerning

To let CorelDraw evenly set the leading:

1. Select the text object with the Shape Tool (**Figure 35**).

2. Position the mouse over the arrow at the lower left corner of the text object.

3. Press the left mouse button and drag the mouse down to add more space between lines (**Figure 36**) or up to decrease the space between lines (**Figure 37**).

or

1. Select the text object with the Pick Tool.

2. Open the Format Text dialog box by selecting Format Text from the Text menu or by pressing Ctrl+T on the keyboard.

3. Click the Spacing tab to bring that tab page to the front (**Figure 38**).

4. Enter a number in the Line text box. You can use the drop down list next to the text box to base the line spacing on the percentage of the character height, a specific set number of points, or a percentage of the point size.

5. Click OK.

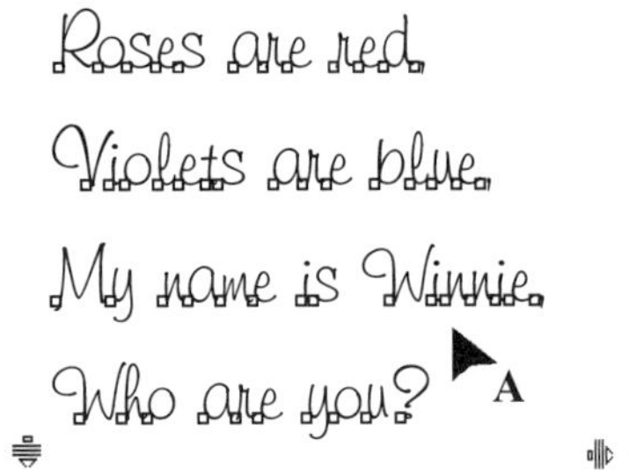

Figure 35. *Select the text object with the Shape Tool.*

Figure 36. *Drag the arrow at the lower left of the text object down to add more space between lines.*

Figure 37. *Drag the arrow at the lower left of the text object up to decrease the space between lines.*

Automatically Set Leading

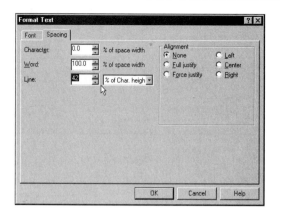

Figure 38. *Use the Spacing tab of the Format Text dialog box to set the amount of space between lines.*

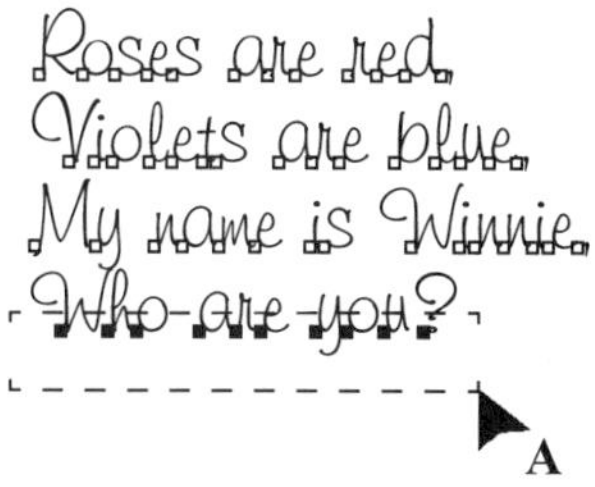

Roses are red,
Violets are blue,
My name is Winnie,
Who are you?
A

Figure 39. *Select several text nodes at once by dragging the Shape Tool to create a marquee.*

To change the leading between individual lines:

1. Select the text block with the Shape Tool.

2. Drag a marquee around the nodes that make up one line (**Figure 39**). This will select them all.

3. Position the mouse pointer over one of the selected nodes, then press the left mouse button and drag the line to its new position (**Figure 40**). As you drag, a dashed blue outline of the line being moved will appear.

4. Release the mouse button. The line of text will redraw in its new position (**Figure 41**).

Roses are red,
Violets are blue,
My name is Winnie,
Who are you?

Who are you?
A

Figure 40. *Press the left mouse button down and drag the selected text nodes to their new position.*

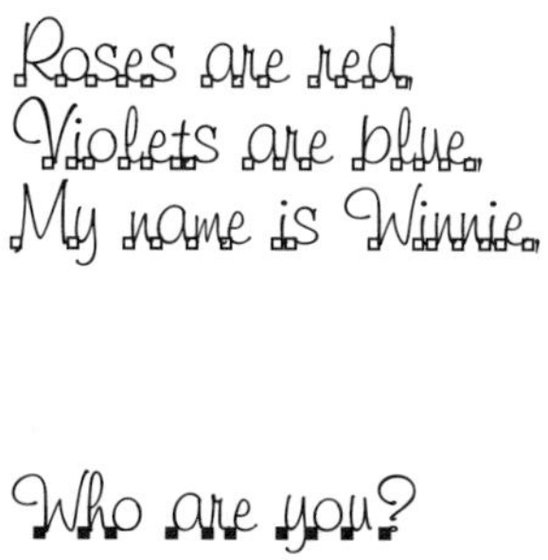

Roses are red,
Violets are blue,
My name is Winnie,

Who are you?

Figure 41. *When you release the mouse, the line of text redraws in the new position.*

Manually Set Leading

*I*f you already have the text for a brochure or newsletter saved in a word processing program, there's no need to retype it into a CorelDraw 7 project. You can import it into the project as paragraph text and manipulate it just as if you were using a page layout program—you can flow text between blocks and around objects, and add bullets and drop caps.

Figure 42. *Use the Import dialog box to select the text you want to bring into a project.*

To import text into a project:

1. Press Ctrl+I on the keyboard or choose Import from the File menu. The Import dialog box will appear (**Figure 42**).

2. Use the Look in drop-down list to move to the folder where the text document is located, and then click on the file name to select it.

3. Click Import.

4. The text will appear in your document in one large text frame (**Figure 43**). You can now work with it like any paragraph text object.

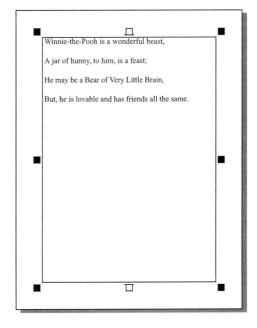

Figure 43. *When the text is imported, it appears in a large text frame.*

TEXT FILE FORMATS

CorelDraw 7 comes with filters that translate text from many word processing programs into CorelDraw paragraph text. To check to see if the word processing program you use can be translated, use the File of type drop-down list found in the Import dialog box (**Figure 42**).

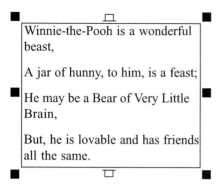

Figure 44. *Select the paragraph text object with the Pick Tool.*

To reshape a paragraph text object:

1. Select the paragraph text object with the Pick Tool (**Figure 44**). Six black handles and two text handles will appear around the object.

2. Drag the handles until the paragraph text object is the desired shape (**Figure 45**).

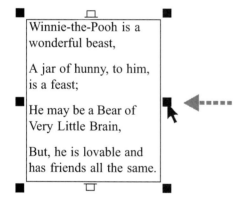

Figure 45. *Drag the handles until the paragraph text object is the right size.*

THE PICK TOOL AND TEXT OBJECT HANDLES

You may have noticed that the Pick Tool affects artistic text objects and paragraph text objects differently. When you drag a handle of an artistic text object, the text changes size and shape. Whereas, when you drag a handle of a paragraph text object, the text stays the same size and rearranges itself depending upon the size of the text frame. To proportionally change the size of paragraph text, hold down the Alt key while dragging a corner handle.

Reshape Paragraph Text

To link text flow between paragraph text frames:

1. Create the paragraph text or import a text file.

2. Select the paragraph text object with the Pick Tool (**Figure 46**). Notice the two text handles, one at the top and one at the bottom of the frame.

3. If you reshape the text object so all the text is not showing, the bottom text handle will change to display a *text flow tab* (**Figure 47**).

4. Position the mouse over the bottom text handle and click. The pointer will change to a page with an arrow attached to it.

5. Position the mouse where you want the paragraph text to continue.

6. Press the left mouse button and drag a new text frame (**Figure 48**). When you release the mouse button, the extra text from the first text frame will flow into the new text frame (**Figure 49**).

Tip:

- You can flow text between paragraph text frames on different pages of text-intensive projects, such as brochures and newsletters. If you add or delete text from a linked paragraph text frame, the text will automatically adjust, flowing between the linked frames.

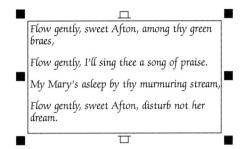

Figure 46. *Select the paragraph text block with the Pick Tool. (Poem by Robert Burns.)*

Figure 47. *If there is more text than the text frame can show, a text flow tab appears in place of the lower text handle.*

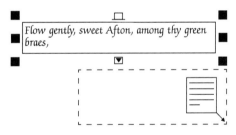

Figure 48. *Position the mouse where you would like the flow of text to appear and drag a new text frame.*

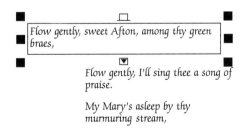

Figure 49. *When you release the mouse button, the text flows into the new text frame.*

Figure 50. *Right mouse click on the closed path object, then select Properties from the pop-up menu.*

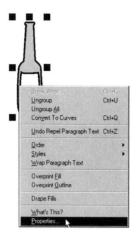

To make new text flow around an object:

1. Make sure the object has a closed path.

2. Select the Pick Tool and right mouse click on the object. A pop-up menu will appear (**Figure 50**).

3. Choose Properties from the menu. The Object Properties dialog box will open.

4. Click the General tab to move that page to the front (**Figure 51**).

5. Put a check in the box before Wrap paragraph text and enter an amount in the Text wrap offset text box.

6. Click OK.

7. Select the Text Tool and drag a text frame around the object (**Figure 52**). A dashed rectangle will appear, showing the text frame and a dashed outline will also appear around the object.

8. Type your text. As you type the text will flow around the object (**Figure 53**).

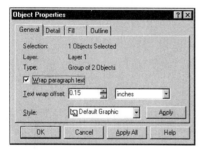

Figure 51. *Use the General tab page of the Object Properties dialog box to set paragraph text wrapping.*

Figure 52. *When you draw a text frame using the Text Tool, a dashed outline also appears around the object.*

Figure 53. *As you type, the text flows around the object.*

Make New Text Flow Around an Object

To make existing text flow around an object:

1. Convert the text object to paragraph text if it is artistic text and select it (**Figure 54**).

2. Make sure the object you want to flow the text around has a closed path, then right mouse click on it with the Pick Tool. Select Properties from the pop-up menu (**Figure 55**).

3. Click on the General tab to move that tab page to the front (**Figure 51**).

4. Put a check in the box before Wrap paragraph text and enter an amount in the Text wrap offset text box.

5. Drag the paragraph text on top of the object. The text will automatically wrap around the object (**Figure 56**).

Tips:

- If you aren't sure whether a text object is paragraph or artistic text, just select it and check the Status Bar.

- You can wrap one paragraph of text around as many objects as you like at a time.

Figure 54. *If the text is artistic, convert it to paragraph.*

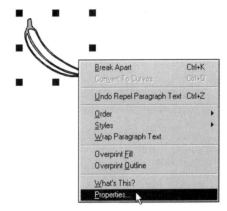

Figure 55. *Right mouse click on the object and select Properties from the pop-up menu.*

Figure 56. *As you drag the paragraph text object over the object, the text rearranges itself around the object.*

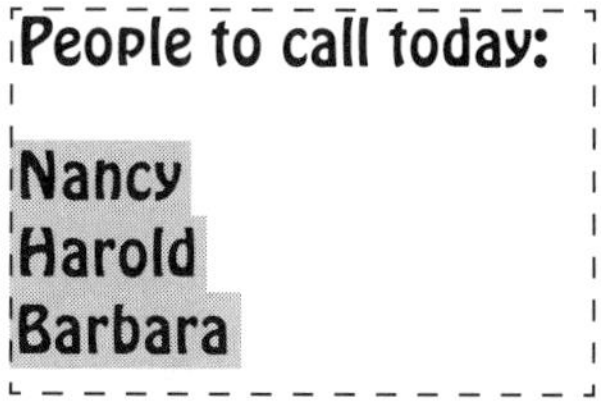

Figure 57. *Use the Text Tool to select the lines of text to which you want to add bullets.*

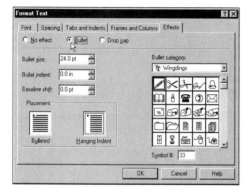

Figure 58. *Select the Bullet option button on the Effects tab page of the Format Text dialog box.*

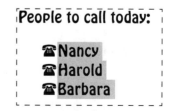

Figure 59. *Select a bullet style from the list and set its size.*

To add bullets to paragraph text:

1. Select the Text Tool, then use it to highlight the text to which you want to add bullets (**Figure 57**).

2. Open the Format Text dialog box by selecting Format Text from the Text menu or pressing Ctrl+T on the keyboard.

3. Click the Effects tab to bring that page to the front (**Figure 58**).

4. Click the option button before Bullet to select it, then choose a bullet style from the list on the right side of the tab page (**Figure 59**).

5. Set the Bullet size and Bullet indent using those text boxes, then click OK. The selected lines of text will redraw with bullets in front of them (**Figure 60**).

Figure 60. *After you click OK, the selected text redraws with bullets.*

Add a Drop Cap to Paragraph Text

To add a drop cap to paragraph text:

1. Select the Text Tool and position it at the beginning of the paragraph where you want the drop cap (**Figure 61**).

2. Open the Format Text dialog box by pressing Ctrl+T on the keyboard or selecting Format Text from the Text menu.

3. Move to the Effects tab page by clicking on the Effects tab.

4. Click the option button before Drop cap to select it, then set how many lines the cap will drop (**Figure 62**).

5. Click OK. The paragraph text will redraw with the dropped cap (**Figure 63**).

Tip:

- You can change the drop cap's font by selecting the character with the Text Tool, then using the Font tab page of the Format Text dialog box.

This paragraph needs some emphasis! A drop cap would be just the thing!

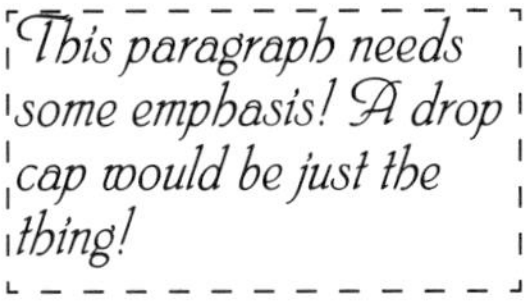

Figure 61. *Place the insertion marker at the beginning of the paragraph where you want the drop cap.*

Figure 62. *Select the Drop cap option button on the Effects tab page.*

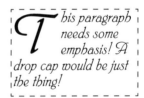

This paragraph needs some emphasis! A drop cap would be just the thing!

Figure 63. *When you click OK, the text redraws with the drop cap.*

SUMMARY:

In this chapter you learned how to:

- Add and edit artistic and paragraph text
- Convert artistic text to paragraph text and vice versa
- Change font, font size, and formatting

- Change character and line spacing
- Import text
- Flow text around objects
- Add bullets
- Add drop caps

Fun with Text

I n the last chapter, you learned how to add text to your projects. This chapter takes text one step further, making it into a design element that enhances your graphics.

This chapter will show you how to *skew* and *rotate* text objects and create shadows. Then you will fit artistic text to a path. From there, you will add *bevels* and *extrusions* to text, then modify characters' shapes. Finally, you will take what you have learned in previous chapters to highlight text with eye-popping neon effects. (You'll have to use your imagination here because the black and white illustrations in this book don't do them justice!)

Skew Text

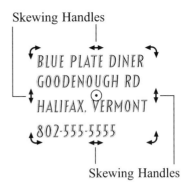

Figure 1. *When you double-click on an object with the Pick Tool, skewing handles appear around its perimeter.*

When a text object is skewed, it is slanted either vertically or horizontally, using *skewing handles* (**Figure 1**). A text object that is rotated is spun around a central point called the *center of rotation marker*, using *rotation handles* (**Figure 4**). Skewing and rotation handles become visible when an object is double-clicked with the Pick Tool. They are double-headed arrows that surround the object in a rectangular formation. The skewing handles are the top, bottom, left, and right center arrows. The rotation handles are the curved arrows at the corners. Rotation and skewing are measured in degrees.

To skew text:

1. Double-click on the text object with the Pick Tool. Double-headed arrows—skewing handles—will appear around the object (**Figure 1**).

2. To skew the text horizontally, position the mouse pointer over the top or bottom skewing handles, then press the left mouse button and drag sideways (**Figure 2**). As you drag, a dashed rectangle appears around the text object and the mouse pointer changes to a double-headed arrow. To skew the text vertically, position the mouse over the left or right skewing handles, then press the left mouse button and drag up or down (**Figure 3**).

Figure 2. *If you drag the top or bottom skewing handle sideways, the text object slants horizontally.*

Figure 3. *If you drag the left or right skewing handle up or down, the text slants vertically.*

Rotation Handle — Center of Rotation Marker — Rotation Handle

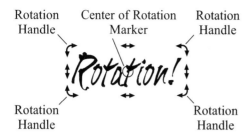

Rotation Handle — Rotation Handle

Figure 4. *Double-click on the text object to make the rotation and skewing handles appear.*

Figure 5. *Drag one of the rotation handles to rotate the text object.*

Figure 6. *Move the center of rotation marker to the position where you want the text object to rotate around.*

Figure 7. *As you drag the text object, notice how it rotates around the center of rotation marker.*

To rotate text:

1. Double-click on the text object with the Pick Tool. The rotation and skewing handles will appear (**Figure 4**). In addition, at the center of the text object, a circle with a dot in the center will appear. This is the center of rotation marker.

2. Position the mouse pointer over one of the rotation handles, press the left mouse button and drag in a clockwise or counterclockwise direction (**Figure 5**). When you drag, a dashed rectangle appears around the text object and the mouse pointer changes to a round double-headed arrow.

3. Release the mouse button. The text redraws in its new, rotated position.

Tip:

■ Experiment with moving the center of rotation marker. To move the marker, place the mouse over it, then press the left mouse button and drag it to a new position (**Figure 6**). Next, rotate the text object and notice how it moves around the marker (**Figure 7**).

ROTATING AND SKEWING OTHER OBJECTS

You can rotate and skew any kind of object—rectangles, polygons, etc.—using the rotation and skewing handles. Just double-click on the object to access the special handles.

Rotate Text

To create text shadows:

1. Use the Text Tool to create some artistic text.

2. Change the typeface to a favorite font using the Font drop-down list on the Property Bar (**Figure 8**). In addition, make the text large enough so it is easy to see. (The font used in Figure 12 is Brush 455 BT.)

3. Open the Options dialog box by pressing Ctrl+J on the keyboard or selecting Options from the Tools menu (**Figure 9**). The dialog box will open with the General tab page in front (**Figure 10**).

4. In the Duplicate placement and nudge area (**Figure 11**), change the Horizontal and Vertical settings to 0.05 inch (0.13 centimeter), then click OK.

Figure 8. *You can use the Property Bar to change the font and font size.*

Figure 9. *Select Options from the Tools menu.*

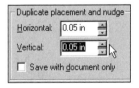

Figure 11. *In the Duplicate placement and nudge area, change both the Horizontal and Vertical settings.*

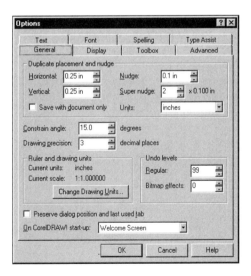

Figure 10. *Use the General tab page of the Options dialog box to set where a duplicate text object will be placed.*

(side text) **Create Text Shadows**

Figure 12. *Select the text object with the Pick Tool.*

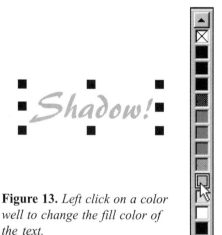

Figure 13. *Left click on a color well to change the fill color of the text.*

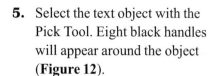

5. Select the text object with the Pick Tool. Eight black handles will appear around the object (**Figure 12**).

6. Change the fill color of the text by left mouse clicking on one of the color wells in the color palette (**Figure 13**). Light gray is a good choice since this text will become the shadow.

7. Duplicate the text object by pressing Ctrl+D on the keyboard or selecting Duplicate from the Edit menu. A duplicate of the text object will appear, selected, slightly up and to the right of the original (**Figure 14**). It may be slightly difficult to see.

8. Change the fill color of the duplicate by clicking the left mouse button on a color well. Pick a color that is darker than the shadow color, bright blue, for instance. You've just created shadowed text (**Figure 15**)!

Figure 14. *The duplicate will appear selected to the right and a little above the original.*

Figure 15. *After clicking the color well to fill the duplicate with a different color, the shadowed text becomes apparent.*

Create Text Shadows

The term *fitting text to a path* means that a line of text is bound to the path of an object. As the text moves along the object's path it assumes the shape of the path. You can fit text to a path interactively or using the Fit Text to Path roll-up.

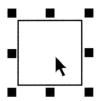

Figure 16. *Use the Pick Tool to select the object to which you want to fit the text.*

To fit text to a path interactively:

1. Select the object to which you want to fit the text with the Pick Tool (**Figure 16**). (The object can have a closed path, or it can be a line.)

Figure 17. *When you click on the selected object's path with the Text Tool, the insertion marker appears at the top of the object.*

2. Select the Text Tool.

3. Position the Text Tool on the object's path. You'll know you're in the right place when the mouse changes from the Text Tool's cross-hair to an I-beam.

Figure 18. *As you type, the text wraps itself around the object.*

4. Click the left mouse button. The insertion marker will appear at the top of the object (**Figure 17**).

5. Type your text. As you type, the text will follow the outline of the object (**Figure 18**).

To fit text to a path using the Fit Text to Path roll-up:

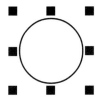

Figure 19. *Create the object to which you want to fit the text.*

1. Create an object to which you want to fit the text (**Figure 19**).

2. Create some artistic text and change it to your favorite font and color (**Figure 20**). (This example is set in the font Pipeline.)

Figure 20. *Create the text you want to fit to the object's path.*

Figure 21. *You can use the Pick Tool to drag a marquee around the two objects to select them.*

Figure 22. *Select Fit Text To Path from the Text menu.*

Figure 23. *Use the Fit Text to Path roll-up to set how the text will bind to the object's path.*

3. Select both objects either by holding down the Shift key while you click or by pressing the left mouse button and dragging to marquee select (**Figure 21**).

4. Select Fit Text To Path from the Text menu (**Figure 22**) or press Ctrl+F on the keyboard. The Fit Text to Path roll-up appears (**Figure 23**).

5. The default settings are fine for a good start, so click Apply. The text will redraw, following the path of the object (**Figure 24**).

Tips:

- Once the text is fit to the path, CorelDraw 7 treats the two objects as one.

- Experiment with the different settings in the drop-down lists in the Fit Text to Path roll-up. The first drop-down list sets the appearance of the text—whether it stands up straight or appears to rotate. The second drop-down list sets the vertical positioning of the text in relation to the object—whether it's above the object, centered on the object's outline, below the outline, or offset by a specific distance.

Figure 24. *When you click Apply, the text fits itself to the object's path.*

Beveling adds a three-dimensional look to text, making it seem like the text is raised up off the page.

Figure 25. *Create the text you want to bevel.*

To create beveled text:

1. Use the Text Tool to create some artistic text.

2. Change the text to a favorite font and increase the font size so the text is easy to see (**Figure 25**). You may also need to zoom in on the text. (The text for this example is set in Arial Black.)

3. With the text object selected, add an outline color to the text by right clicking on a color well. This will add contour lines to the bevels you are about to create.

4. Select Extrude from the Effects menu (**Figure 26**) or press Ctrl+E on the keyboard. The Extrude roll-up will open.

5. Click on the tab with the small color wheel on it to change to the Fill and Shade tab page (**Figure 27**).

6. Add a check to the box next to Use Extrude Fill for Bevel.

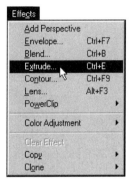

Figure 26. *Select Extrude from the Effects menu.*

Figure 27. *Use the Fill and Shade tab page of the Extrude roll-up to set the bevel color.*

Figure 28. *Click the Shade option button then use the From and To drop-down lists to select bevel colors.*

Figure 29. *Use the Bevel tab page to set the Bevel depth and Bevel angle.*

Figure 30. *When you click Apply, the text redraws with a shaded bevel.*

7. Select the Shade option button, then use the drop-down list to select the From and To shade colors (**Figure 28**). A good setting for the From color is the same color with which the text is filled. White is a good choice for the To color.

8. In the Extrude roll-up, click the next tab to the right of the color wheel—the one with the small beveled square on it—to move to the Bevel tab page (**Figure 29**).

9. Place check marks in both the Use Bevel and Show Bevel Only check boxes.

10. Increase the bevel depth to 0.035 inches (0.9 millimeters) using the Bevel depth text box.

11. Change the Bevel angle to 30 degrees.

12. Click Apply. The artistic text will redraw with a shaded bevel (**Figure 30**).

Tip:

- Experiment with different bevel widths and bevel angles. The larger the angle, the more bevel there will be. However, you will probably want to keep your bevels less than 55 degrees because deeper bevels often look ugly and are impossible to read.

E̤xtrusions make two-dimensional objects appear as if they had three dimensions. When an extrusion is applied to an object, CorelDraw 7 extends points from the object, then joins them to create an extruded surface. This is represented on the screen with dashed lines. From there, the surface is projected out toward a *vanishing point*, represented by an X. The extruded surface and vanishing point combine to give the appearance of depth to the original object.

Figure 31. *Select the artistic text object with the Pick Tool.*

Figure 32. *When the Extrude roll-up opens, dashed lines representing the extended points and extrusion surface appear around the object.*

To extrude text:

1. Use the Text Tool to create some artistic text.

2. Change the text to the desired font, font size, and fill color. (Figure 31 uses the font Cancun.)

3. Right mouse click on a color well—black is a good choice—to add an outline to the text. This will add contour lines to the extrusion you are about to create.

4. Select the text object with the Pick Tool (**Figure 31**).

5. Open the Extrude roll-up by selecting Extrude from the Effects menu (**Figure 26**) or pressing Ctrl+E on the keyboard. When the roll-up opens, dashed lines representing the extended points and extrusion surface will appear around the text object (**Figure 32**).

Figure 33. *Remove the check mark from the box next to Use Bevel on the Bevel tab page of the Extrude roll-up.*

Extrude Text

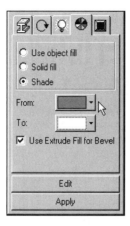

Figure 34. *Use the Fill and Shade tab page of the Extrude roll-up to choose a solid fill or fountain fill for the bevel.*

Figure 35. *On the Extrusion tab page, the defaults for the extrusion setting and vanishing point setting are good for a first try. Change the Depth setting to 10.*

6. Click on the Bevel tab to bring that tab page forward. If there is a check mark in the Use Bevel box, remove it (**Figure 33**).

7. Click the tab with the color wheel on it to move to the Fill and Shade tab page (**Figure 34**).

8. Click either the Solid fill or Shade option buttons. If you choose Solid fill, the extrusion will consist of a solid color. If you select Shade, the extrusion will consist of a blended fountain fill. In either case, select a color for the extrusion using the drop-down list. A good choice is lighter than the fill color of the text.

9. Click on the left-most tab—the one with the extruded I on it—to move to the Extrusion tab page (**Figure 35**).

10. The default extrusion setting—Small Back—and vanishing point setting—VP Locked to Object—are fine. Change the Depth setting to 10 for a first try.

11. Click Apply. The text will redraw with the extrusion (**Figure 36**).

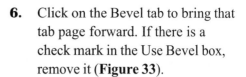

Figure 36. *When you click Apply, the text redraws with the extrusion.*

Extrude Text

To modify character shape:

1. Create some artistic text and select a favorite font. (Figure 37 uses the font OzHandicraft BT.)

2. Select the text object with the Pick Tool (**Figure 37**).

3. Convert the text to curves by pressing Ctrl+Q on the keyboard or selecting Convert To Curves from the Arrange menu (**Figure 38**).

4. Select the Shape Tool. Many, many nodes will appear around the text (**Figure 39**).

Figure 37. *Select the text object with the Pick Tool.*

CONVERTING TEXT TO CURVES

Once text has been converted to curves, you can no longer edit it using the text tool. The reason for this is that CorelDraw 7 "sees" text converted to curves only as closed path shapes—it does not recognize the shapes as text anymore.

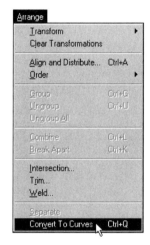

Figure 38. *Select Convert To Curves from the Arrange menu.*

WORKING WITH CURVES

When text is converted to curves, it is like any other object that is made up of curves. It has nodes and can be modified with the Shape Tool. For detailed information about nodes and working with curves, take a look at Chapter 6, *Nodes and Paths*.

Figure 39. *When the text is selected with the Shape Tool after it has been converted to curves, many nodes appear around the perimeter of each letter.*

Modify Character Shape

Figure 40. *Use the Shape Tool to marquee select all the nodes.*

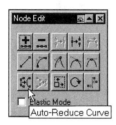

Figure 41. *Click the Auto-Reduce Curve button on the Node Edit roll-up.*

Figure 42. *After you click the Auto-Reduce Curve button, the text shapes redraw with fewer nodes.*

5. Move the mouse to the left and above the text, press the left mouse button, and drag a marquee to select all the nodes (**Figure 40**).

6. Double-click on any node to open the Node Edit roll-up.

7. Click the Auto-Reduce Curve button (**Figure 41**). This will remove a few of the nodes, making the curves easier to work with (**Figure 42**).

8. Click the mouse anywhere outside the text to deselect the nodes.

9. Position the Shape Tool over a node where you would like to alter the shape of the text.

10. Press the left mouse button and drag the node, just as you would reshape any curve (**Figure 43**).

11. Continue moving nodes until the shape of the characters is what you want (**Figure 44**).

Figure 43. *Use the Shape Tool to drag the nodes, just as you would with any object.*

Figure 44. *Continue dragging nodes until you achieve the effect you want.*

Modify Character Shape

Special Project:

The Neon Effect

Figure 45. *Create some artistic text in a favorite font.*

Highlighting text with a bright neon effect is a great way to get attention. All the effect consists of are different color outlines blended together.

To create the neon effect:

1. Create some artistic text and change it to a favorite font in a large point size (**Figure 45**). (Figure 45 uses Brush 738 BT.)

2. Change the text's fill color to red by left mouse clicking on that color well in the Color Palette.

3. Select the text with the Pick Tool and convert it to curves by pressing Ctrl+Q on the keyboard or choosing Convert To Curves from the Arrange menu (**Figure 38**).

4. Click on the Outline Pen button on the Outline Tool fly-out menu (**Figure 46**). The Outline Pen dialog box will open (**Figure 47**).

5. Use the drop-down list next to Color to change the outline color to red, and change the Width to 0.05 inches (1.25 millimeters).

6. Move down the dialog box to the Corners area and select the rounded corner option, and in the Line caps area select rounded caps (**Figure 48**).

7. Put a check mark in the Scale with image box, then click OK.

Figure 46. *Click the Outline Pen button on the Outline Tool fly-out menu.*

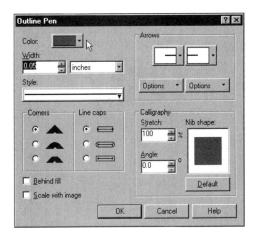

Figure 47. *Use the Outline Pen dialog box to set the outline color, width, corners, and end caps.*

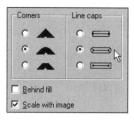

Figure 48. *Click the rounded corners and rounded caps option buttons, then put a check mark in the box next to Scale with image.*

Figure 49. *Click the color well with the X in it to remove the fill from the duplicate.*

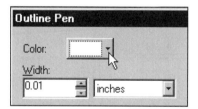

Figure 50. *In the Outline Pen dialog box, use the drop-down list to change the Color to white, then change the Width setting to 0.01 inches.*

Figure 51. *Use the Pick Tool to marquee select both objects.*

8. Select Options from the Tools menu or press Ctrl+J on the keyboard to open the Options dialog box (**Figure 10**).

9. On the General tab page in the Duplicate placement and nudge area, change both the Horizontal and Vertical settings to 0, then click OK (**Figure 11**).

10. With the text object selected, press Ctrl+D on the keyboard or choose Duplicate from the Edit menu. A duplicate of the text object will appear selected directly on top of the original.

11. On the Color Palette, left mouse click the color well with the X in it to remove the fill color from the duplicate (**Figure 49**).

12. Open the Outline Pen dialog box again by clicking the Outline Tool to open the fly-out menu and clicking the Outline Pen button.

13. Use the drop-down list next to Color to change the outline color to white (**Figure 50**).

14. Change the Width setting to 0.01 inches (0.25 millimeters), then click OK.

15. Move the mouse pointer to the left and above the text objects.

16. Press the left mouse button and drag a marquee to select both objects (**Figure 51**). The Status Bar will read: 2 Objects Selected on Layer 1.

Special Project: The Neon Effect

17. Select Blend from the Effects menu (**Figure 52**) or press Ctrl+B on the keyboard. The Blend roll-up will appear (**Figure 53**).

18. The default Blend setting of 20 steps is a good setting, so all you have to do is click Apply. The outlines of the text objects will blend together, creating the neon effect (**Figure 54**).

Figure 52. *Select Blend from the Effects menu.*

Tip:

- You can apply the same techniques to lines and other objects such as the rectangle surrounding the summary box below.

Figure 53. *The default settings on the Blend tab page of the Blend roll-up are good for creating the neon effect, so all you have to do is click Apply.*

Figure 54. *When you click Apply, the outlines of the two objects blend together, creating the neon effect.*

Special Project: The Neon Effect

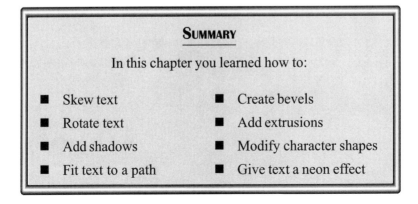

SUMMARY

In this chapter you learned how to:

- Skew text
- Rotate text
- Add shadows
- Fit text to a path

- Create bevels
- Add extrusions
- Modify character shapes
- Give text a neon effect

Layers 13

When two objects are drawn, CorelDraw 7 automatically *stacks* the second object on the first. When a third object is drawn, it is stacked on the second, and so on. This positioning is called the *stacking order*. If the objects do not overlap, the stacking order isn't apparent (**Figure 1**). But, if they do overlap, it's easy to see (**Figure 2**).

You've probably noticed the Status Bar displaying messages such as "Rectangle on Layer 1." By default, CorelDraw 7 places all objects on one *layer*. Layers are invisible planes that stack vertically, one on top of the other (**Figure 3**). Layers help keep a drawing's distinct elements separate. You can add as many layers as you need to a project.

Figure 1. *When objects don't overlap, the stacking order is not apparent.*

Figure 2. *As soon as the objects overlap, the stacking order is easy to see.*

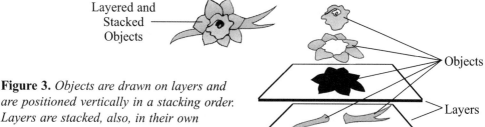

Layered and
Stacked
Objects

Objects

Layers

Figure 3. *Objects are drawn on layers and are positioned vertically in a stacking order. Layers are stacked, also, in their own stacking order.*

You can manipulate the stacking order of objects using the Order commands on the Arrange menu (**Figure 4**).

To bring an object to the front:

1. Select the object using the Pick Tool (**Figure 5**).

2. Press Shift+PageUp on the keyboard or choose Order on the Arrange menu to open the fly-out, then select To Front. The object will move to the front (**Figure 6**).

To position an object in front of a specific object:

1. Select the object you want to position using the Pick Tool (**Figure 7**).

2. On the Arrange menu, choose Order to open the fly-out, then click In Front Of. The mouse pointer will change to a large black, right-facing arrow.

3. Position the black arrow over the object you want to place the selected one in front of and click. The selected object will move in front of the clicked object (**Figure 8**).

To bring an object forward one object:

1. Select the object using the Pick Tool.

2. Choose Order from the Arrange menu, then select Forward One on the fly-out menu.

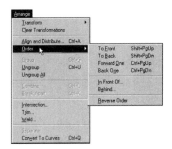

Figure 4. *Use the Order fly-out on the Arrange menu to change the stacking order of objects.*

Figure 5. *Select the object.*

Figure 6. *When you select To Front, the object moves to the front of the stack.*

Figure 7. *Select the object you want to position.*

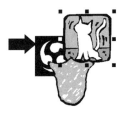

Figure 8. *The selected object moves in front of the object you click with the black arrow.*

Bring an Object Forward

Figure 9. *Select the object you want to send to the back.*

Figure 10. *When you select To Back, the object moves to the back of the stack.*

Figure 11. *Select the object you want to position.*

Figure 12. *The selected object moves behind the object you click with the black arrow.*

To move an object behind all objects:

1. Select the object using the Pick Tool (**Figure 9**).

2. Press Shift+PageDown on the keyboard or select Order from the Arrange menu, then choose To Back on the fly-out. The object will move to the back (**Figure 10**).

To position an object behind a specific object:

1. Select the object you want to position with the Pick Tool (**Figure 11**).

2. Choose Order from the Arrange menu, then select Behind from the fly-out. The mouse pointer will change to a large black, right-facing arrow.

3. Place the black arrow over the object you want to place the selected one behind and click. The selected object will move behind the clicked one (**Figure 12**).

To move an object back one object:

1. Select the object using the Pick Tool.

2. Choose Order from the Arrange menu, then select Back One on the fly-out.

Send an Object Back

171

*U*sing the Layers roll-up, you can create individual layers to work on (**Figure 13**). The settings for a layer determine whether it can be seen, printed, or drawn on, and whether it is a *master layer*. A master layer is used for multiple page documents, where you want the same graphics to appear in the same place on each page. For instance, if you were designing a company newsletter, you could place the company logo on every page automatically by placing the logo on a master layer.

You can create as many layers as you want, and you can change the stacking order of the layers using the Layers roll-up.

The Layers Roll-up

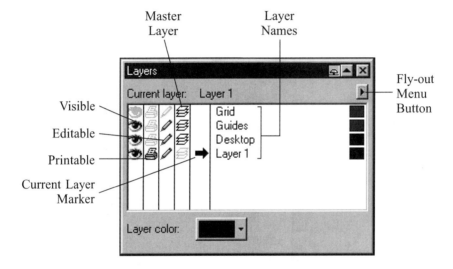

Figure 13. *The Layers roll-up.*

To open the Layers roll-up:

Select Layer Manager from the Layout menu (**Figure 14**) or press Ctrl+F3 on the keyboard.

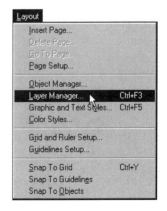

Figure 14. *Select Layer Manager from the Layout menu.*

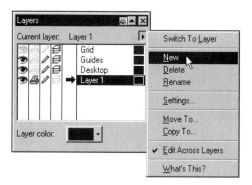

Figure 15. *Select New from the fly-out menu.*

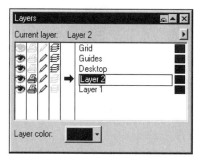

Figure 16. *The new layer appears above the topmost layer.*

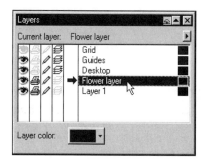

Figure 17. *When you double-click a layer's name, it becomes the current layer.*

To create a new layer:

1. Click the small arrow on the right side of the Layers roll-up. This will open a fly-out menu (**Figure 15**).

2. Select New. The new layer will appear above the topmost layer in the Layers roll-up (**Figure 16**).

3. Type a name for the layer.

4. Press Enter on the keyboard.

To change the Current layer:

Double-click the name of the layer you want to make current. The Current layer marker will move to point at the layer's name (**Figure 17**). Any objects you create will be added to that layer.

WHAT'S THIS? HELP

Remember that What's This? help is always there for you. If you want to find out what something does, just right mouse click on it and choose What's This? from the pop-up menu.

Make a New Layer; Change the Current Layer

To change a layer's settings:

1. Select the layer you want to change by clicking on it (**Figure 18**).

2. Click the small arrow to open the fly-out menu and select Settings. A Settings dialog box for that layer will open (**Figure 19**).

3. Use the Layer name text box to re-name the layer, if you wish. Then move down the box placing check marks in the boxes of the features you want to select: Visible, Printable, Editable, and Master layer.

4. Click OK.

or

Click the appropriate icon to the left of the layer whose settings you want to change (**Figure 20**). If the icon is grayed out, then that setting is turned off.

Tips:

■ Notice that there are Grid and Guides layers. The default color for these layers is blue. If you want grids or guidelines to appear in another color, such as red or black, select the layer and use the Layer color drop-down list near the bottom of the roll-up to select a new color.

■ If you finish with a layer and do not want to inadvertently move any objects on that layer, remove the check mark from the Editable box in the layer Settings dialog box.

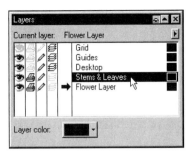

Figure 18. *Select the layer whose settings you want to change.*

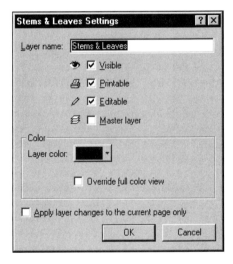

Figure 19. *Use the Settings dialog box to change the layer's capabilities.*

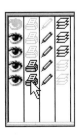

Figure 20. *Click the appropriate icon to change the setting.*

Change Layer Settings

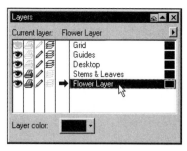

Figure 21. *Position the mouse over the layer you want to move.*

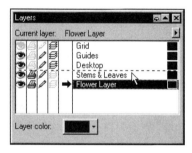

Figure 22. *A dashed line appears as you drag, indicating the layer's possible new position.*

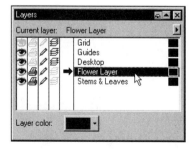

Figure 23. *When you release the mouse button, the layer moves to its new position.*

To reorder layers:

1. Position the mouse pointer over the layer you want to move (**Figure 21**).

2. Press the left mouse button and drag it up or down the list. A dashed line will appear as you drag (**Figure 22**).

3. Release the mouse when the line is where you want to place the layer. The layer will move to that position (**Figure 23**).

USING LAYERS TO CREATE PLANS

Layers can be very helpful when creating technical plans for items such as buildings, gardens, and cars. For instance, when creating a plan for a house, you could create plumbing, electrical, and framing layers. Drawings of pipes would be placed on the plumbing layer, wiring diagrams would be placed on the electrical layer, and window layouts would be placed on the framing layer.

When it came time to print the plans, you could print one sheet that contained all the layers and print separate pages, one for each layer. That way, you could hand each contractor a page for her particular specialty.

Reorder Layers

To move or copy an object to a different layer:

1. Select the object (or objects) with the Pick Tool (**Figure 24**).

2. Click the little arrow on the Layers roll-up to access the fly-out menu and select Move To or Copy To, depending on which you wish to do (**Figure 25**). The mouse pointer will change to a large black arrow.

3. Use the black arrow to click on the layer name to which you want to move the object (**Figure 26**).

Tip:

- Watch the Status Bar—it will always tell you what layer a selected object is on.

To delete a layer:

Select the layer with the Pick Tool then right mouse click. A pop-up menu will appear (**Figure 27**). Choose delete.

Figure 24. *Select the object you want to move to another layer. In this example, the leaf is selected.*

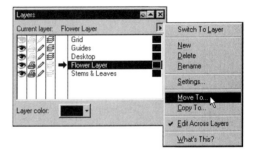

Figure 25. *Select Move To from the fly-out menu.*

Figure 27. *Select Delete from the pop-up menu.*

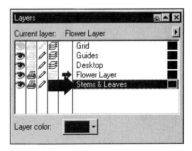

Figure 26. *Use the large black arrow to click on the layer to which you want to move the object.*

Move Between Layers; Delete a Layer

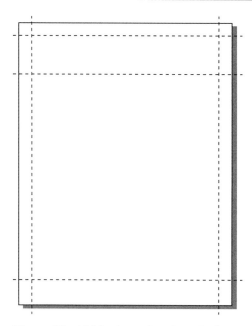

Figure 28. Add horizontal and vertical guidelines to mark the page margins.

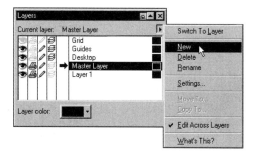

Figure 29. Create a new layer by choosing New from the fly-out menu.

Special Project:

Set Up a Newsletter with Logo

*C*reating a master layer makes all the difference when you set out to create a document that will use the same graphics on every page.

To set up a newsletter:

1. Start a new document by pressing Ctrl+N on the keyboard or selecting New from the File menu (see page 23).

2. Add three horizontal guidelines to the page to mark the page margins, placing the first 0.5 inch down from the top, the next 2 inches from the top, and the third 1 inch from the bottom. Then add two vertical guidelines for the right and left margins, positioning each one 0.5 inch from the edge of the page (**Figure 28**).

3. Open the Layers roll-up by selecting Layer Manager from the Layout menu or by pressing Ctrl+F3 on the keyboard.

4. Add a new layer to the project by clicking the little arrow on the right side of the roll-up and choosing New from the fly-out menu (**Figure 29**).

5. Type the name "Master Layer," then press Enter.

Special Project: Set Up a Newsletter

6. Click the Master Layer icon to make this layer a master layer (**Figure 30**). Notice that the Current layer is Master Layer. This means that any objects you add will go onto the master layer.

7. Add a logo to the upper left corner of the page above the guideline that is 2 inches from the top of the page (**Figure 31**). This example uses a piece of clipart, a finch, from the third CorelDraw 7 CD-ROM. If you want to use it, the finch is located under Clipart\Birds\Songbrds\Finch2.Cdr.

8. Draw a straight line, using the Freehand Tool, along the horizontal guideline below the logo (see page 80).

9. Draw another horizontal line at the bottom of the page where the vertical guidelines intersect with the horizontal guideline.

10. Use the Text Tool to type the date. Center that text below the lower horizontal line. At this point, your page should look something like the one in **Figure 32**.

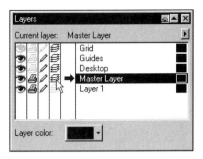

Figure 30. *Click the Master Layer icon to make the new layer a master layer.*

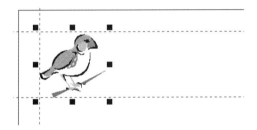

Figure 31. *Add a logo to the upper left corner of the page between the two horizontal guidelines.*

January 9, 1997

Figure 32. *The full page with all the items needed on the master layer.*

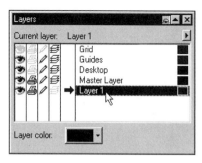

Figure 33. *Double-click Layer 1 to make that layer the Current layer. Any objects added after this change will be placed on Layer 1.*

Figure 34. *Use the Text Tool to add a title next to the logo.*

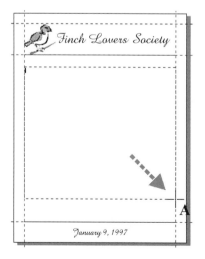

Figure 35. *Use the Text Tool to drag a paragraph text frame from one vertical guideline to the other.*

11. On the Layers roll-up double-click Layer 1 to make it the current layer (**Figure 33**). Any object you add from now on will be added to Layer 1.

12. Move back to the top of the page and create a title for the newsletter with the Text Tool. Use a favorite font and size the text to fit the space next to the logo (**Figure 34**).

13. Add a page to the document (see page 97). Notice that the document moves to that page and that the finch, the two horizontal lines, and the date are visible on the page, but the newsletter title is not present.

14. Move back to page 1 (see page 99).

15. Select the Text tool and drag a paragraph frame that is the width of the page from vertical guideline to vertical guideline (**Figure 35**).

16. Open the Format Text dialog box by selecting Format Text from the Text menu or pressing Ctrl+T on the keyboard.

Special Project: Set Up a Newsletter

17. Click the Frames and Columns tab to move to that tab page (**Figure 36**).

18. Change the Number of columns to 3 and set the Gutter width to 0.5 inch. Click the option button next to Maintain current frame width, then click OK. Three columns with 0.5 inch gutters will appear within the paragraph text frame (**Figure 37**).

19. Type your newsletter text and add a drop cap to the first paragraph, if you desire (see page 152). Use the paragraph frame's text flow tab to flow text onto page 2 (see page 148).

Tip:

■ You can add many elements to a newsletter such as dividing lines between columns, page numbers, and pictures to accompany articles.

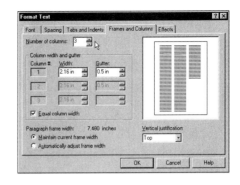

Figure 36. *Use the Frames and Columns tab page to set up three columns for your newsletter text.*

Figure 37. *As you type the newsletter text, it will flow from column to column.*

Special Project: Set Up a Newsletter

SUMMARY

In this chapter you learned how to:

■ Bring objects to the front   ■ Create layers

■ Bring an object forward one   ■ Change layer settings

■ Send objects to the back   ■ Create a master layer

■ Send an object back one   ■ Set up a newsletter

Transformations

It's amazing what you can do with a few clicks of the mouse. The transformation commands—group, combine, rotate, mirror, scale, clone, and blend—are among the most powerful and easy to use tools in CorelDraw 7.

In this chapter you will learn how to group objects and use the combine command to create cut-outs. Next, you will discover the Scale and Mirror roll-up and use it to change an object's size and flip an object vertically and horizontally. From there, the chapter will move on to rotating and cloning objects, and then finish with a special project that shows you how to create the "Woodcut" effect.

Transformation Commands

CHANGING MORE THAN ONE OBJECT AT A TIME

Any of the transformations discussed in this chapter, such as grouping, rotating, sizing, mirroring, etc., can be performed on more than one object or group of objects at a time. Just select the objects you want to change and follow the steps outlined in this chapter.

*G*rouping objects binds them together so they can be manipulated as a unit. For instance, if you want to move several objects yet keep them in the same positions relative to each other, you would group the objects, then move them as a unit. Another use for grouping is formatting. Any type of formatting applied to grouped objects will effect all the objects in the group. For example, you could add a blue fill to all the objects in a group just by selecting the group, then clicking the blue color well on the Color Palette.

Figure 1. *Marquee select the objects you want to group.*

To group objects:

1. Select the objects with the Pick Tool by either holding down the Shift key while clicking on the objects or pressing the left mouse button down to drag a marquee (**Figure 1**).

2. Select Group from the Arrange menu (**Figure 2**) or press Ctrl+G on the keyboard.

Figure 2. *Select Group from the Arrange menu.*

To ungroup objects:

1. Select the grouped objects with the Pick Tool.

2. Choose Ungroup from the Arrange menu (**Figure 3**) or press Ctrl+U on the keyboard.

Figure 3. *Select Ungroup from the Arrange menu.*

Group Objects; Ungroup Objects

Figure 4. *The Rotation roll-up.*

Figure 5. *Select the object using the Pick Tool.*

Figure 6. *To open the Rotation roll-up, select Rotate from the Transform fly-out on the Arrange menu.*

Figure 7. *Enter a number in the Angle text box, then click Apply or Apply To Duplicate.*

Figure 8. *The object redraws rotated.*

hapter 12 showed you how to use the rotation handles to rotate a text object (see page 155). You can use the same techniques—double-clicking to reveal the rotation handles then dragging to rotate—on any object or group of objects. CorelDraw 7 also provides a Rotation roll-up (**Figure 4**) for precision.

To rotate an object:

1. Select the object using the Pick Tool (**Figure 5**).

2. Choose Rotate from the Transform fly-out on the Arrange menu (**Figure 6**). The Rotation roll-up will open.

3. Enter the number of degrees you want to rotate the object in the Angle text box.

4. If you want to rotate the object using one of its handles as the center of rotation, click the small down arrow near the bottom right of the roll-up. The bottom of the roll-up will expand to expose check boxes that correspond to the object's eight black handles (**Figure 7**).

5. Place a check mark in one of these boxes to move the center of rotation.

6. Click either Apply To Duplicate to rotate a duplicate of the original object or Apply to rotate the original object. The object or its duplicate will rotate (**Figure 8**).

Rotate an Object

When you *combine* objects, the lines and shapes fuse to create new shapes and any overlapping areas are removed, creating *clipping holes* that let you see what's underneath.

A perfect use for the combine transformation is the popular black/white graphic effect. With this effect, half of the drawing is white on black and the other half is black on white. (Check out the border on page 181.)

To create a black/white graphic:

1. Create a closed path object and fill it with black by clicking on the black color well in the Color Palette (**Figure 9**). You can use the same graphic shown in this example by opening the Symbols roll-up and selecting image # 61 from the Animals1 collection.

2. Use the Rectangle Tool to draw a rectangle that covers the right half of the graphic (**Figure 10**).

3. Fill the rectangle with black. The rectangle will obscure the graphic beneath it (**Figure 11**). (As you learned in the last chapter, the second object drawn is automatically stacked on top of the first object.)

4. Select the Pick Tool, press the left mouse button, and drag a marquee to select both objects (**Figure 12**).

Figure 9. *Create a closed path object.*

Figure 10. *Use the Rectangle Tool to draw a rectangle that covers half the object.*

Figure 11. *Fill the rectangle with black.*

Figure 12. *Use the Pick Tool to drag a marquee to select both objects.*

Figure 13. *Select Combine from the Arrange menu.*

5. Select Combine from the Arrange menu (**Figure 13**) or press Ctrl+L on the keyboard. The half of the graphic covered by the rectangle will become a cut-out (**Figure 14**).

6. Finish the drawing by creating a matching rectangle for the left side of the image. Send it to the back (press Shift+PageDown on the keyboard) and fill it with white (**Figure 15**).

7. Marquee select all the objects and group them by pressing Ctrl+G on the keyboard or selecting Group from the Arrange menu (**Figure 2**).

Figure 14. *The half covered by the rectangle becomes a cut-out.*

Tips:

- To add another interesting effect to the drawing, create a large square that completely covers the grouped objects. Send the square to the back of the stack (press Shift+PageDown), then fill it with a color such as blue or red, or a texture fill (see page 131). The cut-out, created by the combined objects, lets the large square's fill shine through (**Figure 16**).

Figure 15. *A second rectangle added to the left, filled with white, and sent to the back of the stack finishes the drawing.*

Figure 16. *A filled square placed behind the drawing adds interest.*

- Experiment using these same techniques on text. Create some artistic text, add a color fill, then position a colored rectangle over half the text. Select the two objects and combine them (**Figure 17**).

Figure 17. *You can use the same techniques on artistic text.*

To separate objects that have been fused with the Combine command, use the *Break Apart* command. Break Apart is the exact opposite of Combine.

To break objects apart:

1. Select the combined objects with the Pick Tool (**Figure 18**).

2. Choose Break Apart from the Arrange menu (**Figure 19**) or press Ctrl+K on the keyboard. The objects will resume their original shape (**Figure 20**). You can now work with them as individual objects.

Figure 18. *Select the combined objects.*

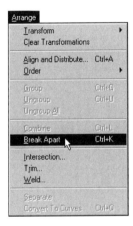

Figure 19. *Select Break Apart from the Arrange menu.*

WORKING WITH CLIPART IMAGES

Many clipart images are created by grouping and/or combining several objects. By ungrouping or breaking these graphics apart, you can modify clipart to suit your needs and taste. Once you've made changes, you can regroup or recombine the graphics.

You can check to see if a graphic has been combined or grouped by selecting the drawing with the Pick Tool, then opening the Arrange menu. If ungroup and/or break apart are available, then the graphic has been grouped and/or combined.

Figure 20. *The objects redraw in their original form.*

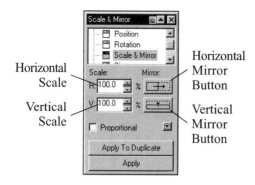

Figure 21. *The Scale & Mirror roll-up.*

Horizontal Scale

Vertical Scale

Horizontal Mirror Button

Vertical Mirror Button

Drag Here

Or Drag Here

Figure 22. *Select the object you want to mirror, then drag either the center left or center right handle.*

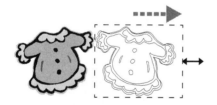

Figure 23. *When you press the Ctrl key and drag the handle, the object flips horizontally.*

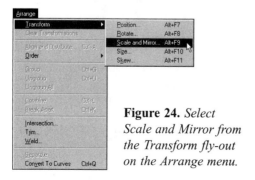

Figure 24. *Select Scale and Mirror from the Transform fly-out on the Arrange menu.*

Mirroring an object flips it vertically or horizontally (or both). You can mirror objects using their handles or using the Scale & Mirror roll-up (**Figure 21**).

To mirror an object horizontally:

1. Select the object with the Pick Tool. Eight black handles will appear around the object (**Figure 22**).

2. Press the Ctrl key while dragging either the left center or right center handle sideways (**Figure 23**). The object will flip horizontally.

or

1. Select the object with the Pick Tool.

2. Select Scale and Mirror from the Transform fly-out on the Arrange menu (**Figure 24**) or press Alt+F9 on the keyboard. The Scale & Mirror roll-up will open (**Figure 21**).

3. Click the Horizontal Mirror button, then click Apply To Duplicate to leave the original object and mirror a duplicate, or click Apply to flip the original object.

Mirror an Object Horizontally

187

To mirror an object vertically:

1. Select the object with the Pick Tool (**Figure 25**).

2. Press the Ctrl key while dragging either the top center or bottom center handle up or down (**Figure 26**). The object will flip vertically.

or

1. Select the object with the Pick Tool.

2. Open the Scale & Mirror roll-up by pressing Alt+F9 on the keyboard or choosing Scale and Mirror from the Transform fly-out on the Arrange menu (**Figure 24**).

3. Click the Vertical Mirror button, then click either the Apply To Duplicate button or the Apply button (**Figure 21**). In **Figure 27**, Apply To Duplicate has been clicked.

Tip:

■ You can easily create a border like the one at the bottom of this page by rotating and mirroring duplicates of original objects. In this case, duplicates of two fish have been mirrored and rotated several times.

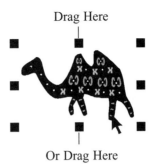

Drag Here

Or Drag Here

Figure 25. *Select the object with the Pick Tool, then drag either the top center or bottom center handle.*

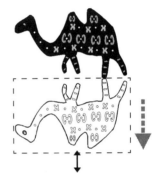

Figure 26. *When you drag the top handle down past the bottom of the object, it flips vertically.*

Figure 27. *After the Apply To Duplicate button is clicked, a copy of the original appears flipped vertically.*

Mirror an Object Vertically

Figure 28. *Select the object you want to scale.*

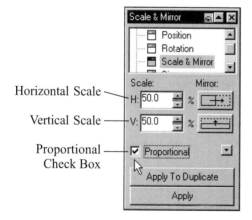

Horizontal Scale

Vertical Scale

Proportional Check Box

Figure 29. *Enter the percentage you want to scale the object to in the H and V text boxes.*

Figure 30. *The original object scaled down by 50%.*

caling an object makes its vertical or horizontal dimension (or both) larger or smaller. In Chapter 4, you learned how to use an object's handles to scale it (see page 46). But, you can also use the Scale & Mirror roll-up to resize objects with more accuracy.

To scale an object:

1. Select the object with the Pick Tool (**Figure 28**).

2. Open the Scale & Mirror roll-up by pressing Alt+F9 on the keyboard or selecting Scale and Mirror from the Transform fly-out on the Arrange menu (**Figure 24**).

3. Enter the horizontal or vertical percentage to which you want to scale the object in the text boxes next to H and V. 100% represents the current size of the object, whereas 50% would be half the size and 200% would be twice the size. You can scale an object both horizontally and vertically at the same time.

4. To change the object's horizontal and vertical scales equally, put a check mark in the check box next to Proportional (**Figure 29**).

5. Click either the Apply To Duplicate button to scale a duplicate of the original or the Apply button to scale the original object. The object or its duplicate will redraw in its new size (**Figure 30**).

Scale an Object

ou've already learned how to duplicate an object in Chapter 4 (see page 45). Like duplication, *cloning* bypasses the Windows 95 Clipboard to quickly create a copy of the original. However, unlike duplication—where the two objects only look alike and are not connected in any other way— cloning creates a link between original and copy. Any changes made to the original also affect the clone.

Figure 31. *Use the Pick Tool to select the object you want to clone.*

To clone an object:

1. Select the object with the Pick Tool (**Figure 31**).

2. Choose Clone from the Edit menu (**Figure 32**). A clone of the original will appear selected (**Figure 33**).

Tips:

- The link between a clone and the original only goes one way. If you alter the original, the clone is changed also. But, if you alter the clone, the original is unaffected.

- You can keep an eye on whether you've selected a clone or the original by watching the Status Bar. If a clone is selected, it will state something such as "Clone Curve on Layer 1." If the original is selected, the Status Bar will read something such as "Control Curve on Layer 1."

- If you group or ungroup cloned objects, any links to the original objects will be cut.

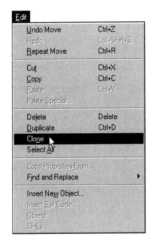

Figure 32. *Select Clone from the Edit menu.*

Figure 33. *A clone of the original appears, by default, above and to the right of the original.*

Clone an Object

Horizontal   Vertical
Setting   Setting

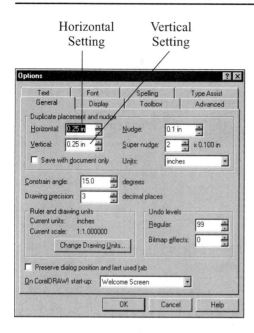

Figure 34. *Use the Duplicate placement and nudge area found on the General tab page of the Options dialog box to set exactly where duplicates and clones will be placed.*

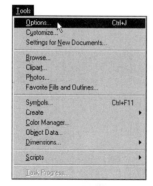

Figure 35. *To access the Options dialog box, select Options on the Tools menu.*

n important dialog box that you have used several times already is the Options dialog box (**Figure 34**). On the General tab page, you can set precisely where a clone or duplicate will appear in relationship to the original, using the Duplicate placement and nudge area.

To set precisely where a clone or duplicate will appear:

1. Select Options from the Tool menu (**Figure 35**) or press Ctrl+J on the keyboard. The Options dialog box will open with the General tab page in front.

2. Enter the distance you want cloned or duplicated objects to appear from the original by typing numbers in the Horizontal and Vertical text boxes. If you want the copy to appear exactly on top of the original, enter 0 in both text boxes.

3. Place a check mark in the box next to Save with document only to save these changes only with this document.

4. Click OK.

Tips:

■ You can quickly create patterns by setting the distances in this dialog box and duplicating or cloning one object.

■ The default horizontal and vertical settings are both 0.25 inch.

Duplicate and Clone Settings

Special Project:

Create the Woodcut Effect

Figure 36. *Triangles are used to create the woodcut-look shadow on the left side of this candle.*

The woodcut look is a very popular highlighting/shadowing technique that is easy to create with CorelDraw 7 (**Figure 36**). All it really consists of are simple triangles that are blended and then grouped together.

To create the woodcut effect:

1. Right mouse click on the Polygon tool and select Properties from the pop-up menu. The Options dialog box will open with the Toolbox tab page in front and Polygon Tool selected.

2. Under Polygon tool defaults, make sure Polygon is selected and Number of points is set to 3 (**Figure 37**), then click OK.

3. Select the Polygon Tool.

4. Press the left mouse button and drag the mouse diagonally to draw a long thin triangle (**Figure 38**).

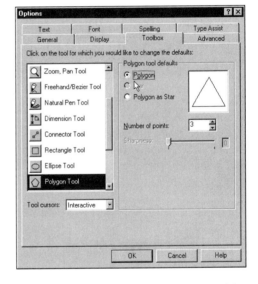

Figure 37. *Use the Toolbox tab page of the Options dialog box to set the Polygon tool default to a polygon with 3 points.*

Figure 38. *Drag the mouse diagonally to draw a long thin triangle using the Polygon Tool.*

Special Project: The Woodcut Effect

Figure 39. *Use Duplicate on the Edit menu or press Ctrl+D on the keyboard to create a copy of the original triangle.*

5. Use the Pick Tool to select the triangle and either choose Duplicate from the Edit menu or press Ctrl+D on your keyboard. A duplicate triangle will appear selected to the right and above the original triangle (**Figure 39**).

6. Drag the duplicate triangle to the right of the original (**Figure 40**).

7. Use Shift+click to select both triangles.

8. Open the Align and Distribute dialog box (**Figure 41**) by pressing Ctrl+A on the keyboard or by choosing Align from the Arrange menu.

9. Put a check mark in the bottom check box to align the triangles to their bottoms, then click OK. The triangles will redraw, aligned (**Figure 42**).

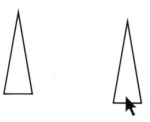

Figure 40. *Use the Pick Tool to drag the duplicate to the right of the original.*

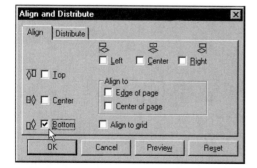

Figure 41. *Click Bottom in the Align and Distribute dialog box, then click OK.*

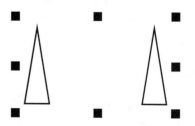

Figure 42. *The bottoms of the triangles are now exactly aligned.*

Next, you need to *blend* the two triangles. Blending creates a specific number of intermediate objects or *steps* between two selected objects. In this case, you are going to use a blend to create several triangles between the two selected triangles.

To blend the two triangles:

1. With both triangles still selected, choose Blend from the Effects menu (**Figure 43**) or press Ctrl+B on the keyboard. The Blend roll-up will open with the Blend tab page in front (**Figure 44**).

2. Make sure the Number of steps option button is selected, and then enter a small number in the text box. **Figure 44** shows 5 as the number of steps.

3. Click Apply. The number of steps you entered will appear between the two selected triangles (**Figure 45**). For the woodcut effect, the triangles should overlap near the bottom. If your triangles do not overlap at all, add more steps using the Blend roll-up. If you have too many triangles and they overlap up near the top points, use the Blend roll-up to reduce the number of steps.

Tip:

■ Keep an eye on the Status Bar. After blending the triangles it will state, "Blend Group on Layer 1."

Figure 43. *Choose Blend from the Effects menu or press Ctrl+B on the keyboard.*

Figure 44. *The Blend roll-up is used to create any number of intermediate objects, or steps, between two selected objects.*

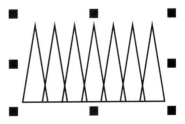

Figure 45. *After clicking Apply, there are several intermediate triangles that overlap each other.*

Special Project: The Woodcut Effect

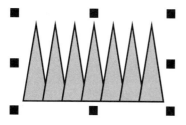

Figure 46. *Fill the triangles with a color that compliments the object you are shadowing or highlighting.*

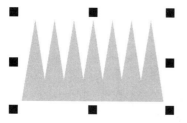

Figure 47. *Right mouse click the color well with an X in it to remove the triangles' outlines.*

Add
Highlights
Here

Figure 48. *Look at the graphic you want to highlight or shadow and figure out how the grouped triangles need to be rotated and scaled.*

inishing the woodcut effect is easy. The final steps involve grouping and filling the triangles with a uniform color, then rotating and scaling them.

To finish the woodcut effect:

1. With all the triangles selected, choose Group from the Arrange menu (**Figure 2**) or press Ctrl+G on the keyboard.

2. Click a color well in the Color Palette to fill the grouped triangles with color (**Figure 46**). To create a woodcut highlight, add a fill to the grouped object that is a few shades lighter than the object being highlighted. To create a shadow, add a fill that is a few shades darker.

3. Right mouse click the color well with the X in it. This will remove the outline from the grouped triangles (**Figure 47**).

4. Look at the object to which you are going to add the woodcut effect and judge how the triangles need to be rotated and scaled (**Figure 48**).

ADDING COLOR TO OBJECTS

It's easy to add a uniform color to objects. Just select the objects and click the color well of your choice. For more information about filling objects with color, see page 120.

5. Rotate (see page 183) and scale (see page 189) the grouped triangles to the appropriate size, then add them to the graphic (**Figure 49**).

Tips:

- If the sides of the grouped triangles need to bend to give the impression of a rounded shape, convert the triangles to curves (see page 62) then use the Shape Tool to manipulate their nodes.

- You can add woodcut highlights and shadows to many kinds of graphics. In addition, extra triangles can be used to create the illusion of three dimensional shape or for adding emphasis (**Figures 50a–c**).

Figure 49. *Add the rotated and scaled triangles to the graphic.*

Figures 50a–c. *Woodcut-look triangles can be added to many styles of graphics.*

Special Project: The Woodcut Effect

SUMMARY

In this chapter you learned how to:

- Group and ungroup objects
- Rotate objects
- Combine and break objects apart
- Scale and Mirror objects

- Clone objects
- Set where clones and duplicates will be placed
- Create a Woodcut effect

Special Effects

Previous chapters showed you how to transform objects with such techniques as duplicating, filling graphics with color and patterns, skewing, grouping, and blending. This chapter takes those transformations and helps you put them together to create exciting special effects. These effects are not hard to do, now that you know the basics, and they will add a professional touch to your graphics. As you move through the chapter, don't hesitate to experiment! If you think a technique you learned previously might add an interesting effect, try it out.

This chapter starts out showing you how to use *envelopes*, containers that distort an object's shape, creating nifty effects. Then, you will use a tool that is new to version 7 of CorelDraw, the *Interactive Blend Tool*, to morph one object into another. From there, you will learn how to create objects by drawing their shadows. Finally, you'll find out how to add motion trails to objects, giving objects the illusion of motion.

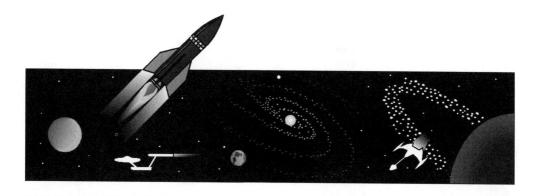

nvelopes are used to distort the shape of objects. An envelope works like a container placed around an object. The object is forced to take on the shape of the container, becoming distorted in the process. The shape of an envelope is manipulated using the Shape Tool and the nodes that appear at various points around the envelope itself.

Figure 1. *Use the Pick Tool to select the object you want to shape.*

Figure 2.
Choose Envelope from the Effects menu.

To shape an object with an envelope:

1. Select the object you want to shape with the Pick Tool (**Figure 1**).

2. Choose Envelope from the Effects menu (**Figure 2**) or press Ctrl+F7 on the keyboard. The Envelope roll-up appears (**Figure 3**).

3. Select the envelope mode you want to use by clicking the appropriate button on the roll-up:

   ■ Straight-line—a straight line is maintained between each of the corner nodes (**Figure 4a**)

   ■ Single-arc—a curved line is allowed between each pair of corner nodes (**Figure 4b**)

   ■ Double-arc—a wavy line is allowed between each pair of corner nodes (**Figure 4c**)

   ■ Unconstrained—you can edit the envelope path, dragging nodes and control points, as if it were an outline drawn with the Freehand or Bézier Tools (**Figure 4d**)

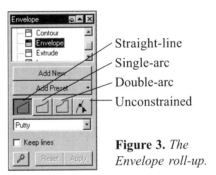

Straight-line
Single-arc
Double-arc
Unconstrained

Figure 3. *The Envelope roll-up.*

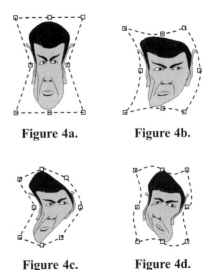

Figure 4a.   **Figure 4b.**

Figure 4c.   **Figure 4d.**

Shape an Object with an Envelope

Figure 5. *When you click the Add New button, a dashed rectangle and nodes appear around the object.*

4. Click the Add New button. An envelope, represented by eight nodes connected by a dashed red line, appears around the object (**Figure 5**). The Shape Tool is automatically selected.

5. Drag the nodes with the Shape Tool until the envelope is the desired shape (**Figure 6**).

Figure 6. *Use the Shape Tool to drag the nodes and shape the envelope. (This is a straight-line mode envelope.)*

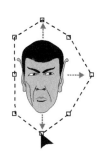

6. Click Apply. The graphic redraws, using the envelope container to reshape it (**Figure 7**).

Tips:

- When working in unconstrained mode, you can add nodes, change node types, and manipulate the envelope's outline just like any ordinary path, using the Shape Tool and Node Edit roll-up (for more about nodes see Chapter 6).

Figure 7. *After you click Apply, the object redraws, using the envelope to reshape it.*

- You can also create an envelope that mimics a shape, In **Figure 8**, the bottle outline was placed behind the face. The face was then selected and an unconstrained mode envelope was added around the face. The next step was to shape the envelope like a bottle, using the bottle outline as a guide. When Apply was clicked the face squashed into the bottle.

- If you want to put several objects in an envelope, you must group them first.

Figure 8. *Vulcan in a bottle...fascinating.*

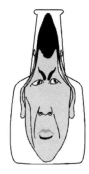

Special Project:

Shape an Envelope like an Object

In chapter 6, you learned how to make a heart by manipulating a circle's nodes. You can add special emphasis to that heart by adding the word "love" to the heart in a heart-shaped envelope.

To add the word "love" to a heart:

1. Create the heart as described in Chapter 6 (**Figure 9**).

2. Use the Text Tool to type the word "LOVE." Choose a favorite font and size the text to the width of the heart (**Figure 10**). (The font used in this example is Apollo MT.)

3. Select the text with the Pick Tool, then open the Envelope roll-up by pressing Ctrl+F7 on the keyboard or by choosing Envelope from the Effects menu (**Figure 2**).

4. On the Envelope roll-up click the Add Preset button to display a list of pre-designed envelope shapes. Scroll down the list until you find the heart shape (**Figure 11**).

Figure 9. *Create a heart.*

Figure 10. *Create the word "LOVE," then size it to the width of the heart.*

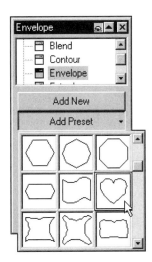

Figure 11. *Select the heart-shaped envelope from the drop-down list of presets.*

Figure 12. *When you click the preset heart shape, a heart-shaped envelope appears on top of the text.*

Figure 13a. *Drag the envelope's nodes and control points to shape the envelope, using the heart as a guide.*

Figure 13b. *Continue draging nodes and control points until you have achieved a heart shape.*

Figure 14. *When you click Apply, the text redraws using the heart-shaped envelope as a container.*

5. Click the heart shape. A small heart-shaped envelope will appear around the text (**Figure 12**).

6. Using the envelope's nodes and control points, reshape the envelope using the heart you created earlier as a guide (**Figures 13a–b**).

7. Click apply. The text will redraw, spreading out to the edges of the heart-shaped envelope (**Figure 14**). Fill the heart with a favorite color (red is always a good choice for a heart), then fill the type with another color (**Figure 15**).

Tip:

■ To modify an envelope after Apply has been clicked, select the enveloped object, click Add New on the Envelope roll-up, then click Reset. The envelope will appear in its last edited form.

Figure 15. *Add your favorite fill colors to the heart and enveloped text.*

Special Project: Envelope Shaping

Blends create a specific number of intermediate objects, or steps, between two selected objects. You can use a blend to quickly create several copies of the same object—which you did in the last chapter when creating the woodcut effect—or to blend two different objects together to create a morph.

Figure 16. *Select the two objects you want to blend.*

To blend two objects together using the new Interactive Blend Tool:

1. Select the two objects you want to blend with the Pick Tool (**Figure 16**).

2. Select the Interactive Blend Tool (**Figure 17**). Three tiny pages and an arrow will attach to the mouse pointer.

3. Position the mouse over the first object, press the left mouse button, and drag over to the second object. A dashed arrow will appear as you drag (**Figure 18**).

4. Release the mouse button. The blended steps will appear between the two objects (**Figure 19**).

Tip:

- You can use the Property Bar to increase or decrease the number of steps created by the Interactive Blend Tool (**Figure 20**).

Figure 17. *Select the Interactive Blend Tool from the Toolbox.*

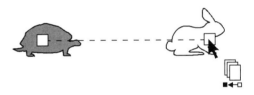

Figure 18. *Drag the Interactive Blend Tool from the first object to the second.*

Figure 19. *When you release the mouse button, blended objects appear between the original objects.*

Number of Steps

Figure 20. *You can use the Property Bar to change the number of steps.*

Figure 21. *Use the Pick Tool to select the two objects.*

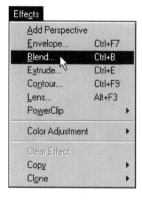

Figure 22. *Choose Blend from the Effects menu.*

Figure 23. *Use the Blend tab page of the Blend roll-up to set the number of steps, angle of rotation, and whether the blend objects will loop.*

To blend objects using the Blend roll-up:

1. Select the two objects with the Pick Tool (**Figure 21**).

2. Choose Blend from the Effects menu (**Figure 22**) or press Ctrl+B on the keyboard. The Blend roll-up will open with the Blend tab page in front (**Figure 23**).

3. Enter the number of steps you would like blended between the two objects and type a number in the Rotate text box to make the blended objects move in a circular fashion.

4. If you want the blended objects to move in an arc, put a check mark in the box next to Loop.

5. Press Apply. The blended objects will appear between the two selected objects (**Figure 24**).

Figure 24. *When you click Apply, the blended objects appear between the two selected ones.*

Use the Blend Roll-Up

203

*S*hadows make drawings appear more realistic, as if they were three dimensional. One use for shadows is understated emphasis. You can use shadows to create the outline of an object that is filled with the same color as the background (**Figure 25**).

Figure 25. *A shadow can be used to create text or any other object.*

To create an object defined by its shadow:

1. Select Options from the Tools menu to open the Options dialog box.

2. On the General tab page in the Duplicate placement and nudge area, change the value in the Nudge text box to 0.01 inch (**Figure 26**) and click OK.

Figure 26. *Change the Nudge setting to 0.01 inch (0.025 centimeter).*

3. Select the object you want to shadow with the Pick Tool (**Figure 27**).

4. Fill it with the same color you will use for the background, and right mouse click on the color well with the X in it to remove the object's outline (**Figure 28**). (This example uses 30% black for the background and object fill.)

Figure 27. *Select the object you want to define with its shadow.*

5. Select Copy from the Edit menu or press Ctrl+C on the keyboard. This copies the object to the Windows 95 clipboard.

Figure 28. *Fill the object with the chosen background color and remove any outline.*

6. Position the mouse pointer over the object and press the right mouse button. Drag the wireframe version of the object down and to the right of the original object (**Figure 29**).

Figure 29. *Use the right mouse button to drag a copy of the object.*

Figure 30. *Click Copy Here on the pop-up menu.*

7. Release the mouse button. A pop-up menu will appear asking whether you want to copy or move the object. Select Copy Here (**Figure 30**).

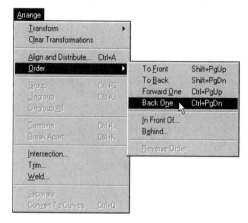

8. Press Ctrl+PageDown on the keyboard or select Back One from the Order fly-out on the Arrange menu (**Figure 31**). This moves the copied object behind the original object.

9. Use the Pick Tool to select the original object.

Figure 31. *Select Back One from the Order fly-out on the Arrange menu.*

10. Change the original object's fill color to a color that is a few shades darker than the original color (**Figure 32**). (This example uses 60% black.)

11. Drag a marquee to select both objects (**Figure 33**).

12. Open the Blend roll-up by pressing Ctrl+B on the keyboard or by choosing Blend from the Effects menu.

13. Set the Number of steps to 40 and enter 0 in the Rotate text box.

Figure 32. *Change the original object's color to a few shades darker than the background color.*

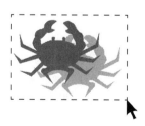

Figure 33. *Drag a marquee to select the two objects.*

Create a Shadow Object

14. Click Apply. The two objects blend together (**Figure 34**).

15. Press Ctrl+V on the keyboard or select Paste from the Edit menu. A copy of the original object appears selected.

16. Left mouse click in the white color well to fill the copy with white (**Figure 35**).

17. You need to nudge the white filled copy up and slightly to the left to create a highlight. To do this, you are going to use CorelDraw's built in nudge feature. Press the up arrow key ⬆ once to nudge the object up 0.01 inch. Then press the left arrow key ⬅ once to nudge the object left 0.01 inch. You may not even notice the object move.

18. Press Ctrl+V on the keyboard or select Paste from the Edit menu again. Another copy of the original appears (**Figure 36**).

19. Use the Rectangle Tool to draw a rectangle that is larger than the objects you've just created. Fill the rectangle with the background color you originally decided on.

20. Position the rectangle directly over the objects you have made.

21. Press Shift+PageDown on the keyboard to send the rectangle to the back of the stack or choose To Back from the Order fly-out on the Arrange menu (**Figure 37**).

Figure 34. *When you click Apply, the two objects blend together.*

Figure 35. *Fill the copy with white.*

Figure 36. *Choosing Paste from the Edit menu creates another copy of the original object.*

Figure 37. *After adding a rectangle filled with the background color, the object's shadow becomes apparent.*

Create a Shadow Object

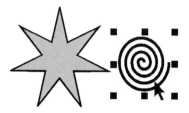

Figure 38. *Select the object you want to use as the "contents."*

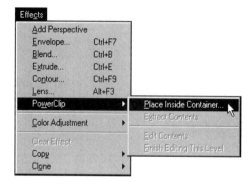

Figure 39. *Choose Place Inside Container from the PowerClip fly-out on the Effects menu.*

Figure 40.
When you click on the container object, the contents object redraws inside it.

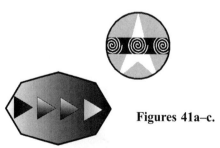

Figures 41a–c.

You can put one object inside another using the PowerClip command. When you use PowerClip, one object becomes a container, while the other object becomes the contents. Any part of the contents that does not fit in the container gets "clipped" off.

To powerclip two objects:

1. Select the object you want to use as the "contents" with the Pick Tool (**Figure 38**).

2. Choose Place Inside Container from the PowerClip fly-out on the Effects menu (**Figure 39**). The mouse pointer changes to a large black arrow.

3. Click on the container object. The contents object will redraw inside the container object (**Figure 40**).

Tips:

- The container object can be any closed path object you create in CorelDraw, such as stars, polygons, and artistic text.

- The contents object can be any object created in CorelDraw or any imported object, such as bitmap images. (For more about bitmaps, see Chapter 16.)

- Let your imagination soar when using the PowerClip command! You never know what will look interesting together (**Figures 41a–c**).

Create PowerClipped Objects

The Lens roll-up (**Figure 42**) lets you simulate the effects created by camera lenses, including fish eye, brightening, transparency, and color inversion. Any closed path object, such as a square, star, or artistic text object, can be used as the lens that views the drawing behind it.

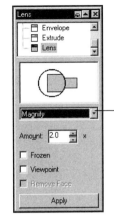

Figure 42. *The Lens roll-up lets you add interesing viewing effects.*

Lens Type Drop-Down List

To add a lens effect to a graphic:

1. Choose Lens from the Effects menu (**Figure 43**) or press Alt+F3 on the keyboard.

2. Select the object that is going to become the lens with the Pick Tool and position it on top of the graphic that will be viewed with the lens (**Figure 44**).

3. Use the Lens Type drop-down list on the Lens roll-up to select a lens effect.

4. Click Apply. The lens graphic redraws, completing the effect on the graphic behind it (**Figure 45**). Try out the different lenses available on the Lens Type drop-down list (**Figure 46a–c**).

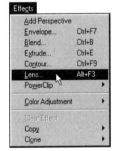

Figure 43. *Choose Lens from the Effects menu.*

Figure 44. *Position the lens object on top of the graphic to be viewed.*

Figure 45. *The star viewed through a magnifying lens.*

Figure 46a. *A fish eye lens.*

Figure 46b. *A transparency lens.*

Figure 46c. *A brightening lens.*

Add Lens Effects

Figure 47. *Select the clipart rocket from the Scrapbook roll-up.*

Figure 48. *Resize the rocket and zoom in so you can see it clearly.*

Figure 49. *On the General tab page of the Options dialog box, use the Duplicate placement and nudge area to change the Horizontal setting to -2.0 inches and the Vertical setting to 0.*

Special Project

Making Drawings Move

howing motion is hard when all you have is a still page. Motion blurs, which are fading trails behind objects, help give the impression of motion. These trails are simply blends.

This example uses a clipart rocket, available on CorelDraw 7 CD-ROM disk 3 as Clipart\Space\Rockets\Rocket8.Cdr.

To make a rocket fly:

1. Import the clipart rocket using the Scrapbook roll-up (**Figure 47**). (For more about importing clipart see page 215.)

2. Resize the rocket so it is about 3 inches (7.6 centimeters) long and zoom in to see it clearly (**Figure 48**).

3. Select the rocket and ungroup it by pressing Ctrl+U on the keyboard or by choosing Ungroup from the Arrange menu. The Status Bar will state "17 Objects Selected on Layer 1."

4. Open the Options dialog box by selecting Options from the Tools menu.

5. In the Duplicate placement and nudge area of the General tab, change the Horizontal setting to -2.0 inches (5 centimeters) and the Vertical setting to 0 (**Figure 49**), then click OK.

6. Select the upper black, rocket fin, then choose Duplicate from the Edit menu or press Ctrl+D on the keyboard. A duplicate fin will appear 2 inches to the left of the rocket (**Figure 50**).

Figure 50. *The duplicate tail fin appears 2 inches to the left of the rocket.*

7. Notice that the bottom edge of the duplicate fin is curved. That edge needs to be straight so that it follows the straight red tube of the rocket. Drag a horizontal guideline down and align it exactly with the edge of the red rocket tube (**Figure 51**).

8. Choose Snap to Guidelines from the Arrange menu, then select the Shape Tool.

Figure 51. *Add a horizontal guideline, aligning it with the top edge of the red rocket tube.*

9. Zoom in so you can see the duplicate tail fin clearly, then click on it with the Shape Tool to select it. Nodes will appear around the fin (**Figure 52**).

10. Drag the nodes on the bottom edge of the fin up to the guideline to straighten it out (**Figure 53**).

11. Zoom out so you can see the rocket again.

Figure 52. *When you select the tail fin copy, nodes appear around its perimeter.*

Figure 53. *Drag the nodes on the bottom of the tail fin copy up to the guideline.*

Figure 54. *Fill the tail fin copy with 30% black and remove the outline.*

Figure 55. *Drag the gray copy on top of the original black tail fin.*

Figure 56. *When the copied tail fins are blended, a fading trail appears.*

12. Select the Pick Tool, then select the tail fin.

13. Fill the fin with 30% black and remove the outline by right mouse clicking on the color well with an X in it (**Figure 54**).

14. Select Copy from the Edit menu or press Ctrl+C on the keyboard.

15. Press Ctrl+V on the keyboard or choose Paste from the Edit menu. A copy of the gray tail fin will appear selected.

16. Use the Pick Tool to drag the gray copy on top of the original rocket tail fin (**Figure 55**).

17. Select the tail fin to the left of the rocket and fill it with the background color.

18. Hold down the Shift key and click on the gray fin that is on the rocket. The Status Bar will read: "2 Objects selected on Layer 1."

19. Open the Blend roll-up by pressing Ctrl+B on the keyboard or by choosing Blend from the Effects menu (**Figure 22**).

20. Set the Number of steps to 30, then click Apply. The gray and background color tail fins will blend, creating a fading trail (**Figure 56**).

21. Choose To Back from the Order fly-out on the Arrange menu or press Shift+PageDown on the keyboard. The blended trail will move behind the black tail fin (**Figure 57**). Congratulations! You just made your first motion trail!

22. Repeat steps 6–21, making a blended trail for the bottom fin (**Figure 58**).

Tip:

■ There are other ways to show motion. You can also create motion trails using lines and curves (**Figures 59a–c**).

Figure 57. *When the blended tail copies are sent to the back of the stack, they become a motion trail.*

Figure 58. *Adding a second motion trail makes the rocket take off!*

Figures 59a–c.

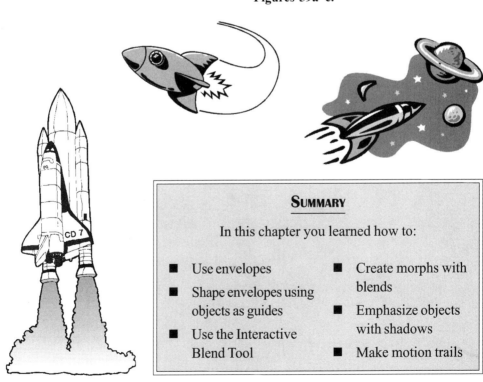

SUMMARY

In this chapter you learned how to:

■ Use envelopes

■ Shape envelopes using objects as guides

■ Use the Interactive Blend Tool

■ Create morphs with blends

■ Emphasize objects with shadows

■ Make motion trails

Clipart and Bitmaps

CorelDraw 7 ships with over 32,000 pieces of clipart. What an amazing library of beautiful images to have at your fingertips! (For the location of all the clipart used in this book, see Appendix A.)

A new feature included in CorelDraw 7 is the ability to create photographic or painterly effects with *bitmaps*. Bitmaps are images made up of tiny dots called pixels. If you zoom in on a bitmap, you will see a pattern of tiny colored squares.

CorelDraw 7 is primarily a vector-based drawing program that gives you all the tools you need to create professional-quality graphics. Throughout this book, you've created vector graphics—drawings made with lines and fills created with mathematical formulas. Now, with the addition of bitmap technology, you can take your drawings one step further, giving them photo-quality realism.

Vector-Based Drawing; Bitmap Images

In CorelDraw, you can add symbols from such symbols fonts as Wingdings and ZapfDingbats to your documents, and manipulate them as you would any other graphical object. In fact, CorelDraw ships with thousands of symbols, organized into collections.

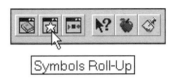

Figure 1. *Click the Symbols Roll-Up button on the Standard Toolbar.*

To add symbols to a document:

1. Click the Symbols Roll-Up button on the Standard Toolbar (**Figure 1**) or select Symbols from the Tools menu (**Figure 2**). The Symbols roll-up will open (**Figure 3**).

2. Use the drop-down list to select a collection of symbols. The collection will appear in the sample window.

3. Scroll down the sample window until you find the symbol you want.

4. Position the mouse over the symbol, press the left mouse button, and drag the symbol on to the drawing window (**Figure 4**). You can now work with the symbol like any other CorelDraw graphic.

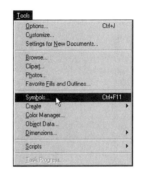

Figure 2. *Choose Symbols from the Tools menu.*

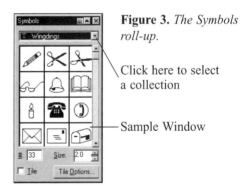

Figure 3. *The Symbols roll-up.*

Click here to select a collection

Sample Window

Tips:

- You can set the size of a symbol using the Size text box.

- If you know the number of the symbol you want to use in a particular collection, just type the number in the # text box. The symbol will appear selected in the sample window.

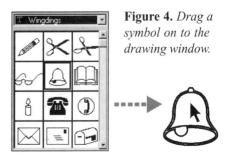

Figure 4. *Drag a symbol on to the drawing window.*

Symbols as Graphical Elements

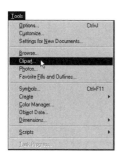

Figure 5. *Choose Clipart from the Tools menu.*

Figure 6. *When the Scrapbook roll-up opens, the Clipart folder is present in the window.*

Figure 7. *Put the correct disk in your CD-ROM drive and click OK.*

Figure 8. *The clipart is organized into categories by folder. Double-click to access the contents of a folder.*

The Scrapbook roll-up makes it easy to import the clipart and bitmaps that ship on the CorelDraw 7 CD-ROM disks.

To import clipart:

1. Select Clipart from the Tools menu (**Figure 5**). The Scrapbook roll-up will open with the Clipart tab page in front (**Figure 6**).

2. If you do not have the correct CD-ROM loaded in your CD-ROM drive, the Find CD dialog box appears (**Figure 7**). Insert the correct CD-ROM disk, then click OK.

3. Use the window on the tab page the same way you would use Windows 95 Explorer. Double-click on the Clipart folder. The contents of the folder—many more folders, organized by category—will appear (**Figure 8**).

4. Scroll down the list of folders until you find one that may contain an item you want to import, then double-click that folder.

5. Use the scroll bar to move down the list of importable files.

Import Clipart

Import Bitmaps

6. When you find a file to import, position the mouse pointer over the item, press the left mouse button, and drag the object onto the page (**Figure 9**).

7. Release the mouse button. The graphic will appear (**Figure 10**).

Tips:

■ Graphics files can be rather large. Importing graphics may use a lot of your computer's resources, slowing it down.

■ When you import an item using the Clipart tab page, the graphic will be grouped. To work with the graphic, ungroup it, then alter it as you please.

To import bitmaps:

1. Choose Photos from the Tools menu. (**Figure 11**). The Scrapbook roll-up will open with the Bitmap tab page in front (**Figure 12**).

2. Double-click on a folder to access its contents.

3. Scroll down the list of importable bitmaps until you find the right one.

4. Position the mouse over the bitmap you want to import, press the left mouse button, and drag it out onto the page (**Figure 9**).

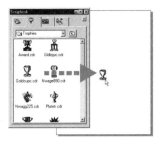

Figure 9. Drag the clipart from the Scrapbook roll-up onto the page.

Figure 10. When you release the mouse, the clipart is added to your project.

Figure 11. Choose Photos from the Tools menu.

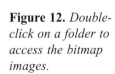

Figure 12. Double-click on a folder to access the bitmap images.

216

Figure 13. *Select the vector drawing with the Pick Tool.*

The new Bitmaps menu offers many interesting tools and *filters* that you can use to manipulate bitmaps. Filters let you add special effects such as blurring, sharpening, and geometric distortions to bitmaps.

Figure 14. *Choose Convert to Bitmap from the Bitmaps menu.*

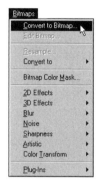

To convert a vector drawing to a bitmap:

1. Select the vector drawing you want to convert with the Pick Tool (**Figure 13**).

2. Choose Convert to Bitmap from the Bitmaps menu (**Figure 14**). The Convert to Bitmap dialog box will open (**Figure 15**).

3. In the Colors area, select the number of colors from the drop-down list and put a check in the Dithered box. *Dithering* will keep the transitions between colors smooth in drawings that contain blends or fountain fills.

4. Select a Resolution using the drop-down list and choose the Normal option button in the Anti-aliasing area. *Anti-aliasing* blends the pixels at the boundaries between colors for a smoother look.

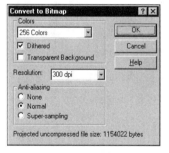

Figure 15. *Use the Convert to Bitmap dialog box to set the bitmap's number of colors and resolution.*

5. Click OK. The drawing will be converted. You may notice some difference in the quality of the converted drawing. Lines may appear dotty since they are being created with pixels (**Figure 16**). (Compare Figure 13 with Figure 16.)

Figure 16. *The bitmapped image may appear more dotty since the lines are now created with pixels.*

Convert a Vector Drawing to a Bitmap

With the auto-trace feature, you can quickly create vector drawings from bitmapped images.

To auto-trace a bitmap:

1. Select the bitmap image with the Pick Tool (**Figure 17**). The Status Bar will display something along the lines of "Color Bitmap on Layer 1."

2. Select the Freehand Tool or Bézier Tool from the Toolbox.

3. Position the mouse over the area you want to auto-trace. The mouse will change to a cross-hair with three dots attached to it.

4. Click the left mouse button. CorelDraw will trace an outline of the area (**Figure 18**).

5. Select the Pick Tool. The traced outline will automatically be selected.

6. Move the outline off the bitmap (**Figure 19**). You can now manipulate the traced outline as you would any other vector graphic.

Tip:

- The auto-trace feature only works on high contrast areas. If an area is made up of similar soft shades, auto-trace will not work.

Figure 17. *Select the bitmap image with the Pick Tool.*

Figure 18. *When you click on an area of the bitmap with the mouse, a tracing of the bitmap is created.*

Figure 19. *Use the Pick Tool to move the traced vector drawing off of the bitmap.*

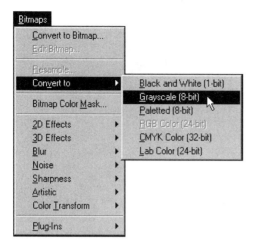

Figure 20. *Choose a color model from the Convert to fly-out on the Bitmaps menu.*

any filters on the Bitmaps menu will not be available unless the selected bitmap is converted to a color model. (Color models are discussed on page 123.) Some available color models include grayscale, RGB, and CMYK. Typically, grayscale is used to display an image in up to 256 shades of gray, RGB is used to display images on a computer monitor, and CMYK is used for color printing.

To convert a bitmap from one color model to another:

1. Select the bitmap with the Pick Tool.

2. Choose Convert to from the Bitmaps menu. A fly-out will appear (**Figure 20**).

3. Select the color model you want to use from the fly-out.

FILE SIZE AND BITMAPS

When choosing the number of colors and resolution for your bitmap, keep in mind that the higher you put the settings, the larger the file will be when saved. The simplest bitmapped image can be quite large (over 1MB) and for larger files, the sky's the limit.

CONVERTING VECTOR DRAWINGS TO BITMAPPED IMAGES

Once a vector drawing has been converted to a bitmap and saved, there's no easy way to convert it back to vector format. You could use the auto-trace feature to recreate the drawing, but that can take time. Instead, save a copy of the drawing before converting it to a bitmap.

Convert Bitmap Color Model

U sing bitmap filters is easy. All you need to do is select the filter from the Bitmaps menu, then move the controls in the dialog box that appears for that specific filter. Two examples—adding an impressionist touch and adding *noise*—are given here to get you started. To see other filter options, check out the filter effects shown on page 222.

Figure 21. *Select the bitmap using the Pick Tool.*

To make a bitmap look like an impressionist painting:

1. Select a bitmap with the Pick Tool (**Figure 21**).

2. Choose Impressionist from the Artistic fly-out on the Bitmaps menu (**Figure 22**). The Impressionist dialog box appears (**Figure 23**).

3. Use the Horizontal and Vertical sliders in the Scatter area to set the effect. The higher the setting, the more the pixels will be scattered.

4. Click Preview to see what you have done (**Figure 24**).

5. If you like what you see, click OK, otherwise click Reset. The bitmap will revert to its original form and you can try other settings.

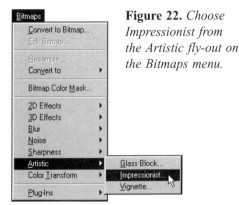

Figure 22. *Choose Impressionist from the Artistic fly-out on the Bitmaps menu.*

Figure 23. *Use the Impressionist dialog box to set the effect.*

Figure 24. *Click Preview to see the effect created by the settings.*

Figure 25. *Select the bitmap with the Pick Tool.*

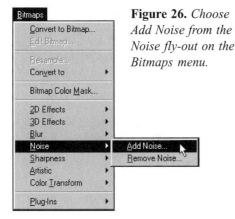

Figure 26. *Choose Add Noise from the Noise fly-out on the Bitmaps menu.*

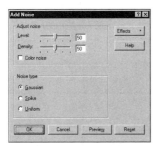

Figure 27. *Use the Add Noise dialog box to set the amount and density of random pixels.*

Figure 28. *Click Preview to see the effect created by the settings.*

The Add Noise filter adds random pixels to a bitmap to give it a speckled appearance. It can be used to simulate a photograph taken on high-speed film.

To add noise to a bitmap:

1. Select a bitmap with the Pick Tool (**Figure 25**).

2. Choose Add Noise from the Noise fly-out on the Bitmaps menu (**Figure 26**). The Add Noise dialog box will open (**Figure 27**).

3. Set the amount of noise in the Adjust noise area, using the Level and Density sliders. In addition, move to the Noise type area and select from the three options: Gaussian, Spike, and Uniform.

4. Click the Preview button to see the effect you have created (**Figure 28**).

5. If the effect is what you want, click OK. Otherwise, click Reset. The drawing will return to its original form.

Tip:

- The three types of noise that you can choose from, Gaussian, Spike, and Uniform, are based on mathmatical formulas. Each formula creates a different pattern of dots that make up the "noise" added to a bitmap.

Add Noise to a Bitmap

Bitmap Filter Effects

BITMAP FILTER EFFECTS

There are many filters that come with CorelDraw 7. You can use them to create interesting painterly effects. The figures below show some of the filters in action.

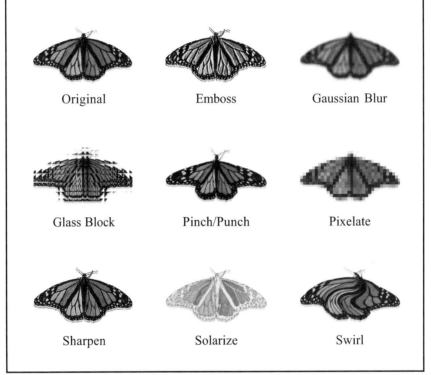

Original	Emboss	Gaussian Blur
Glass Block	Pinch/Punch	Pixelate
Sharpen	Solarize	Swirl

SUMMARY

In this chapter you learned how to:

- Import clipart using the Scrapbook roll-up
- Import bitmaps
- Convert a vector graphic to a bitmap image

- Change a bitmap's color model
- Make a bitmap look like an impressionist painting
- Add noise to a bitmap

Creating Graphics for the Web

The World Wide Web is a train with stops at every house that has a phone line and a modem. More and more people catch that Internet express every day, surfing and creating web pages. With CorelDraw 7 and its new Internet tools, you can jump on board and add graphics to the Web.

In this chapter you will learn how to change the default ruler and resolution settings and load browser color palettes in preparation for designing your graphics. From there, you'll discover how to export your drawings for the Web in both .Gif and .Jpg formats. Finally, you'll take a tour of the new Internet Objects Toolbar and discover how to *map* an image, assign *alternate text*, and publish a page for the Web.

World Wide Web Terms

WORLD WIDE WEB TERMS

- Alternate text—text that appears in the position where the graphic will be while the graphic loads.

- Browser— the program that decodes the information coming across the phone lines, turning it into the World Wide Web pages you see on your computer monitor. The predominant browsers are Microsoft's Internet Explorer and Netscape's Navigator.

- Links—highlighted and usually underlined words on a Web page that transport you to a different Web site or Web page when clicked.

- Map—assign a URL to a graphic or text, creating a link to another site or Web page.

- URL—*Uniform Resource Locator*. A URL is an address for a Web site. An example of a URL is http://www.BearHome.com.

- Web server—a computer connected to the Web that contains Web pages.

$\mathcal{S}$ ince the Web is a visual medium, CorelDraw's settings should be based on what will work for a computer monitor, not a printed page. A monitor uses pixels as its unit of measure and a screen resolution of 72 *dots per inch* (dpi). (A dot equals a pixel.)

To change the rulers to pixels and set resolution:

1. Select Grid and Ruler Setup from the Layout menu (**Figure 1**) or double-click on one of the rulers. The Grid & Ruler Setup dialog box will open with the Ruler tab page in front (**Figure 2**).

2. In the Units area, use the drop-down list next to Horizontal to select pixels.

3. Make sure there's a check mark in the Same units for Horizontal and Vertical rulers check box.

4. Click the Resolution button. The Edit Pixel Resolution dialog box will appear (**Figure 3**).

5. Set the Horizontal resolution to 72.

6. Put a check mark in the Identical values check box, then click OK to return to the Grid & Ruler Setup dialog box.

7. Click OK. The rulers will change to pixels.

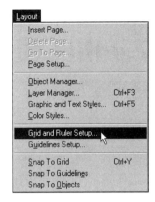

Figure 1. *Choose Grid and Ruler Setup from the Layout menu.*

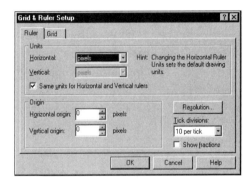

Figure 2. *Set the Horizontal drop-down list to pixels and put a check in the check box next to Same units for Horizontal and Vertical rulers.*

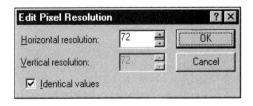

Figure 3. *Set the Horizontal resolution to 72, put a check in the Identical values check box, then click OK.*

Change to Pixels and Set Resolution

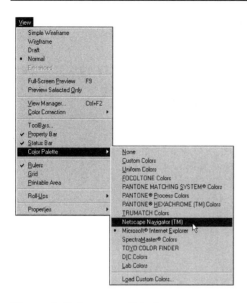

Figure 4. *Select one of the browser palettes from the Color Palette fly-out on the View menu.*

When you design graphics for the Web, you should use the colors that the Web browsers display well. CorelDraw 7 comes with two new color palettes, designed especially for use with Microsoft's Internet Explorer and Netscape's Navigator. You can load either of these palettes into the Color Palette for easy access.

To load browser colors into the Color Palette:

1. Choose Color Palette on the View menu to access the fly-out (**Figure 4**).

2. Select either Netscape Navigator or Microsoft Internet Explorer from the fly-out. You're now ready to create graphics for the Web.

HELP WITH WEB DESIGN

The best source for advice on the Web is the Web itself. There are many sites on the Web that offer advice on Web page design and style. Page design isn't just about pretty pictures, it includes creating user-friendly sites that make it easy for visitors to find the information they need. A few sites that offer interesting advice and tools for Web design are:

Sun Microsystem Inc.'s Guide to Web Style:
http://www.sun.com/styleguide

Web Designer's Paradise:
http://desktoppublishing.com/webparadise.html

Web Style Manual:
http://info.med.yale.edu/caim/StyleManual_Top.html

World Wide Web Consortium:
http://www.w3.org/pub/www/

Load Browser Colors

*O*nce you've created graphics, they need to be exported in file formats that Web browsers can read. You will want to export your graphic as either a .Gif or a .Jpg. (For directions on exporting a file see page 28.)

The .Jpg file format is ideal for photographs and images with depth and small color changes such as lighting effects. When you export a graphic as a .Jpg, a JPEG Export dialog box will appear (**Figure 5**). In this dialog box, you can set the graphic's Quality Factor. The higher the quality the larger the file size. Keep the quality as low as possible (without sacrificing too much of the image's quality) to minimize file size.

The .Gif file format is typically used for black and white art, line drawings, and images that are less than 256 colors. When you export a graphic as a .Gif in CorelDraw, a Transparent Color dialog box will open (**Figure 6**). You will need to specify whether the .Gif should be 87a Format or 89a Format. Here's what those formats do:

- 87a Format (developed in 1987) is the standard .Gif format. This is a good format to use for small images that will load quickly on a Web page. A special feature of this format is that you can create *interlaced* images. An interlaced .Gif file appears on the Web screen in chunks, starting at a low resolution, and progressing after several seconds to its final form.

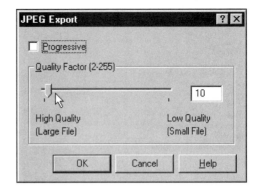

Figure 5. *The JPEG Export dialog box is used to set the image's quality.*

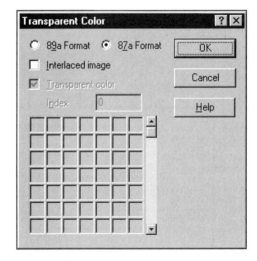

Figure 6. *The Transparent Color dialog box is used to select the .Gif file format and whether the image will be interlaced and/or transparent.*

Exporting Graphics for the Web

DOWNLOADING THE LATEST BROWSERS

You can download the most recent versions of Internet Explorer and Navigator using the Web. Just enter the following URLs and follow the directions you find there.

To download
Microsoft's Internet Explorer, go to:
http://www.microsoft.com/ie/

To download
Netscape's Navigator, go to:
http://www.netscape.com/

- 89a Format (guess when it was developed…you got it—1989) is a descendant of the original .Gif format.

As with its predecessor, the 87a format, 89a format offers the ability to create interlaced images. You can also create *transparent* images, where sections of the image (usually the background) are invisible. This is handy when a Web page has a special background pattern. You don't have to try to match the graphic's background to the background on the Web page (an impossible task!); instead, the image's invisible background lets the Web page background shine through.

Remember that every kilobyte of information takes about one second to load on a Web page, so keep those .Gif and .Jpg files small!

FOR MORE INFORMATION ON CREATING WEB PAGES

There are many books about the Web, and designing and programming Web sites. A few helpful ones with interesting, provocative ideas include:

- *Creating Killer Web Sites* by David Siegel (Hayden Books)
- *<designing web graphics>* by Lynda Weinman (New Riders)
- *Elements of Web Design* by Darcy DiNucci, Maria Giudice, and Lynne Stiles (Peachpit Press)
- *HTML: The Definitive Guide* by Chuck Musciano and Bill Kennedy (O'Reilly & Associates)
- *HTML for the World Wide Web: Visual QuickStart Guide* by Elizabeth Castro (Peachpit Press)

The Internet Objects Toolbar (**Figure 7**) makes it easy to map images and assign alternate text.

Enter URL here

Use outline as edge of graphic

Add bounding box

Foreground color

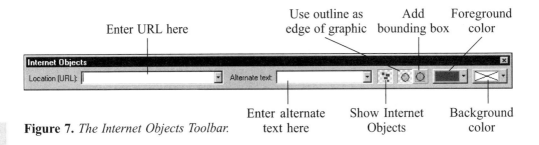

Enter alternate text here

Show Internet Objects

Background color

Figure 7. *The Internet Objects Toolbar.*

To open the Internet Objects Toolbar:

1. Choose ToolBars from the View menu (**Figure 8**). The Toolbars dialog box will open (**Figure 9**).

2. Put a check mark in the check box next to Internet Objects, then click OK. The Toolbar will appear at the center of the screen.

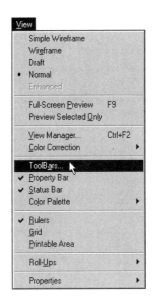

Figure 8. *Choose ToolBars from the View menu.*

Figure 9. *Put a check mark in the check box next to Internet Objects.*

Figure 10. *Select the graphic with the Pick Tool.*

Figure 11. *Assign a URL and alternate text using the Internet Objects Toolbar.*

WHICH OBJECT HAS AN ASSIGNED URL?

If you click the Show Internet Objects button on the Internet Objects Toolbar (**Figure 7**), cross-hatching appears on the objects with assigned URLs.

To assign a URL and alternate text to a graphic:

1. Select the graphic with the Pick Tool (**Figure 10**).

2. In the Location (URL) drop-down list on the Internet Objects Toolbar, type the URL (**Figure 11**).

3. In the Alternate text drop-down list, type the alternate text.

Tips:

- Once you enter a URL or alternate text in the appropriate drop-down list's text box, it will be added to the drop-down list. So if you need that URL or alternate text for another image, just click the little down arrow to open the drop-down list and select it.

- You can also assign URLs and alternate text to artistic and paragraph text. To do so, use the Text Tool to select the words and follow steps 2 and 3.

You can design an entire Web page with CorelDraw, assigning URLs and alternate text to the graphics and text on your page. Then, you can convert that page to Internet-ready files using a new Corel technology called *Barista*. Barista is a technology that completely encapsulates your text and graphics into Internet-ready files. There's no programming involved.

Assign URLs and Alternate Text

To convert a file into Internet-ready format:

1. Choose Publish To Internet from the File menu (**Figure 12**). The Export dialog box will appear (**Figure 13**).

2. Move to the folder where you want to put the files, then type a name in the File name text box.

3. Click Export.

4. If your file contains graphics, the Corel Barista Export dialog box will appear (**Figure 14**). Choose whether you want to export the graphics in the Gif or Jpeg format, then click OK.

Figure 12. *Choose Publish To Internet from the File menu.*

Figure 14. *Select the export file format for your graphics, then click OK.*

Figure 13. *Use the Export dialog box to name the HTML files.*

SUMMARY

In this chapter you learned how to:

- Change the ruler units to pixels
- Set the pixel resolution
- Load browser specific colors into the Color Palette
- Export .Gif and .Jpeg graphics

- Assign URLs and alternate text with the Internet Objects Toolbar
- Publish documents using Barista technology

Printing   *18*

orelDraw 7 stores drawings as mathematical equations and bitmap images as pixels, but both types of graphic are rendered as dots when they are printed. The printed page depends upon the resolution of the output device. The higher the resolution, the finer and sharper the output will be.

For every document you print, you'll need to use the Print dialog box (**Figure 1**). This dialog gives you access to all the print services you need.

Selected Printer

Click here to access printer properties

Use this area to set which pages get printed

Use this area to set how many copies get printed

Click here to access Print Preview mode

Click here to access printing options

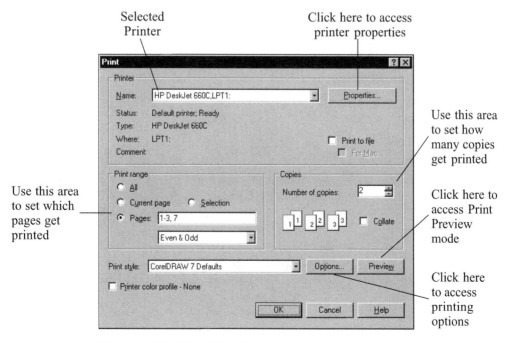

Figure 1. *The Print dialog box.*

To print a document:

1. Choose Print from the File menu (**Figure 2**) or press Ctrl+P on the keyboard. The Print dialog box will open with your default printer selected (**Figure 1**).

2. Click OK to print.

Tip:

■ Always save your document before you print.

To print more than one copy of a document:

1. Select Print from the File menu (**Figure 2**) or press Ctrl+P on the keyboard.

2. In the Copies area to the right of the dialog, type a number in the Number of copies text box or click the little up arrow to increase the number (**Figure 3**)

3. Click OK to print.

Tip:

■ If your document contains more than one page, the Collate check box will be available. Put a check mark in this box to collate multiple copies of a document.

Figure 2. *Select Print from the File menu.*

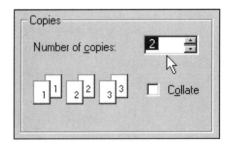

Figure 3. *Use the Number of copies text box to set how many copies of a document will print.*

Figure 4. *In the Print range area of the Print dialog box, you can set which pages to print.*

SETTING PAGE RANGES

If you use the Pages option, you can print specific pages and a page range by specifying page numbers like this: 2, 5, 7–10, 22. If you enter a number followed by a hyphen, for example, 3–, the document will be printed from the specified page to its end.

To print specific pages or objects:

1. Open the Print dialog box by selecting Print from the File menu or by pressing Ctrl+P on the keyboard.

2. Select one of the following option buttons in the Print range area (**Figure 4**):

   ■ All—this option will print the entire document and is the default

   ■ Current page—this option will print the page that is currently viewed on the screen

   ■ Selection—if you selected objects before you opened the Print dialog box, selecting this option will print only those objects

   ■ Pages—you can use the text box next to this option to set the page numbers that will print. Using the drop-down list below this option, you can set whether Even & Odd pages will print or just Even or just Odd.

3. Click OK to print.

Print Specific Pages

If you create a drawing that is larger than the printer can handle, you can use the Layout tab page of the Print Options dialog box to scale the drawing down to fit the printed page, or you can *tile* the printout. You'll know your page is too large for the printer if there are negative numbers in the Top and Left text boxes on the Layout tab page. Tiling splits the drawing onto several pages with overlap areas built in. After printing, you can put the pages together to view the entire drawing at its true size.

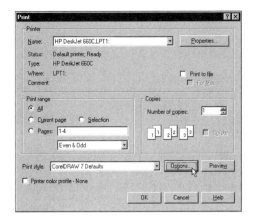

Figure 5. *Click the Options button on the Print dialog box.*

To size or scale a printout:

1. Choose Print from the File menu or press Ctrl+P on the keyboard to open the Print dialog box.

2. Click the Options button at the lower right of the dialog box (**Figure 5**). The Print Options dialog box will open with the Layout tab page in front (**Figure 6**).

3. In the Position and size area, you can set an exact size by typing measurements in the Width and Height text boxes or you can scale the drawing to a percentage, using the Print Scaling text boxes (**Figure 7**). If the Maintain aspect ratio box is checked, the printed image will be scaled proportionately.

4. Click OK to close the Print Options dialog and return to the Print dialog box.

5. Choose more printing options or click OK to print.

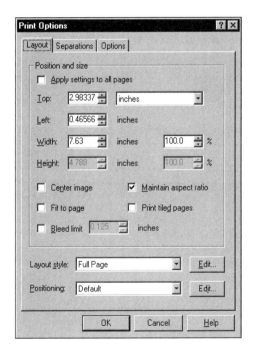

Figure 6. *The Print Options dialog box with the Layout tab page in front.*

Size or Scale a Printout

Set Width Here   Set Scaling Percentages

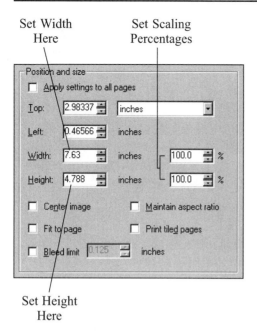

Set Height Here

Figure 7. *Use the Position and size area to size or scale the printed drawing.*

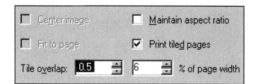

Figure 8. *Enter the amount that you want the tiled pages to overlap.*

To tile a printout:

1. Choose Print from the File menu or press Ctrl+P on the keyboard to open the Print dialog box.

2. Click the Options button at the lower right of the dialog box (**Figure 5**). The Print Options dialog box will open with the Layout tab page in front.

3. Put a check mark in the check box next to Print tiled pages (**Figure 7**). Two text boxes will appear below the check box and the Center image and Fit to page check boxes will become unavailable (**Figure 8**).

4. Enter a precise measurement for the Tile overlap (0.5 inch is a good setting) or enter a percentage number in the text box to the left of % of page width.

5. Click OK to close the Print Options dialog box and return to the Print dialog box.

6. Choose more printing options or click OK to print.

7. When you print the tiled pages, you can piece them together to view the drawing as a whole.

Tile a Printout

OTHER LAYOUT PRINTING OPTIONS

There are two more check boxes that you can select when setting printing layout options: Center image and Fit to page (**Figure 7**). If you put a check mark in the Center image box, CorelDraw 7 will automatically center your drawing on the printed page. If you put a check mark in the Fit to page box, your drawing will be automatically resized to fit the printed page.

Every printer has properties that you can set including, the size and orientation of the paper and resolution it will use, and whether it will print in color (if it's a color printer). You can access these settings in the Print dialog box.

To select a different printer:

1. Choose Print from the File menu or press Ctrl+P on the keyboard to open the Print dialog box. Near the top of the dialog box in the Printer area is a drop-down list next to Name.

2. Click the small arrow at the right to view the drop-down list (**Figure 9**).

3. Select the printer you want to use.

4. Choose more printing options or click OK to print.

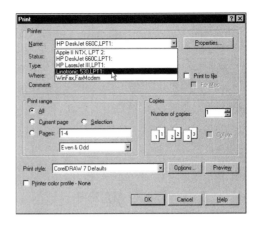

Figure 9. *Use the Name drop-down list in the Print dialog box to select another printer.*

NOT ALL PRINTERS ARE CREATED EQUAL

There are many brands of printers and imagesetters out there in the marketplace, but most of them use only two languages to process printing commands, *PCL* or *PostScript*. Printer Command Language (PCL), developed by Hewlett-Packard, is a printer-dependent language that operates only at the printer level. PostScript, developed by Adobe, is a fully programmable language that can be used to *encapsulate—* completely contain—all the necessary information for printing a document.

Some PCL printers include the DeskJet series by Hewlett-Packard, dot matrix printers, and the Canon BubbleJet series. Some PostScript output devices include the Linotrinic and Varityper imagesetters, and the Apple LaserWriter series printers.

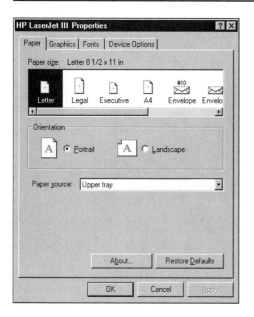

Figure 10. *The Properties dialog box for each printer will be different depending on the printer's capabilities.*

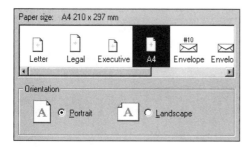

Figure 11. *Click on the paper icon for the size you want. The dimensions of the chosen paper size appear at the top left of the area. To select a page orientation, click either the Portrait or Landscape option buttons.*

To set a different page size and orientation for a printer:

1. Open the Print dialog box by choosing Print from the Options menu or pressing Ctrl+P on the keyboard.

2. Use the Name drop-down list to select a printer (**Figure 9**).

3. Click the Properties button to the right of the Name drop-down list. The Properties dialog box for that printer will open (**Figure 10**). This dialog box will contain different options for different printers depending on the printers' capabilities.

4. If the Paper tab page is not already in front, click the Paper tab.

5. Use the scrolling window under Paper size to select a new size, and use the Orientation area to set whether the page will be printed in a portrait or landscape orientation (**Figure 11**).

6. Click OK to close the Properties dialog box.

7. Choose more printing options or click OK to print.

Set Printer Page Size and Orientation

When preparing files for a service bureau or print shop, you will probably need to generate PostScript (.Ps) or Encapsulated PostScript (.Eps) files, and include crop marks, and information about the project and how you want it printed. If your project is in color, you will need to prepare *color separations*—creating one sheet for each process and spot color—with registration marks (see page 123 for a discussion about color).

Note: Before preparing files for a service bureau or print shop, contact them to find out what file format and printer settings to use.

To add crop and registration marks and file information:

1. Open the Print dialog box by pressing Ctrl+P on the keyboard or selecting Print from the File menu.

2. Click the Options button at the lower right of the dialog box (**Figure 5**). The Print Options dialog box will appear with the Layout tab page in front (**Figure 6**).

3. Click the Options tab to bring that tab page to the front (**Figure 12**).

4. In the Proofing options area, put a check mark in the box next to Fit printer's marks and layout to page (**Figure 13**).

5. To print an information sheet for the printer, put a check in the box next to Print job information sheet.

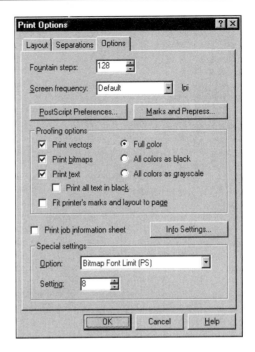

Figure 12. *The Print Options dialog box with the Options tab in front.*

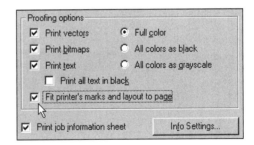

Figure 13. *Put a check in the Fit printer's marks and layout to page, otherwise the printer's marks won't print because they will be outside the printable page boundary.*

PROOFING OPTIONS

In the Proofing options area shown in Figure 13, you can set various options that help you proof a project. These options include:

■ Print vectors: if checked, your vector drawings will print

■ Print bitmaps: if checked, any bitmap images will print

■ Print text: if checked, any text in your project will print

■ Print all text in black: if checked, any colored text will print in black

These options can come in handy if you have a complex document and only want to print proofs of certain elements at one time.

6. Click the Marks and Prepress button. The Printer's Marks and Prepress Settings dialog box will open (**Figure 14**).

7. Put check marks in the check boxes next to the items you want to select as shown in **Figure 14**.

8. Click OK. This will take you back to the Print Options dialog box.

9. Click OK again to return to the Print dialog box. Print the document or save it as a file, or continue choosing printing options.

Put a check here to print registration marks

Put a check here to print file information

Put a check here to print page numbers

Put a check here to print crop marks

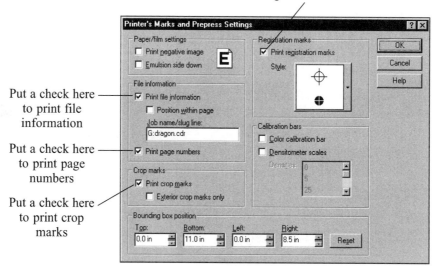

Figure 14. *Use the Printer's Marks and Prepress Settings dialog box to add file information, page numbers, crop marks, and registration marks to your output.*

To create color separations:

1. Choose Print from the File menu or press Ctrl+P on the keyboard to open the Print dialog box.

2. Click the Options button to open the Print Options dialog box.

3. Click the Separations tab to bring that tab page to the front (**Figure 15**).

4. Put a check mark in the check box next to Print separations.

5. Select the colors that you want printed as separations by clicking on the color name (**Figure 16**).

6. Click the Options tab to move to that tab page (**Figure 12**).

7. Click the Marks and Prepress button. The Printer's Marks and Prepress Settings dialog box will open (**Figure 14**).

8. Put a check mark in the check box next to Print file information. This will print the name of each color on its separation page.

9. Put a check mark in the box next to Print registration marks.

10. Click OK to close the Printer's Marks and Prepress Settings dialog box.

11. Click OK again to return to the Print dialog box.

12. You may continue choosing other printing options or click OK to print the separations or save the print job to file for output at a service bureau or print shop.

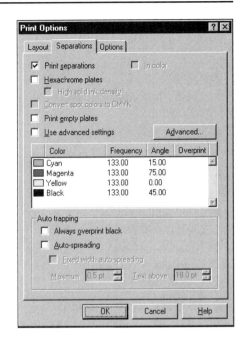

Figure 15. *Use the Separations tab page in the Print Options dialog box to select separations settings.*

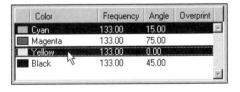

Figure 16. *Click on the color names to select which color separations will be printed.*

Create Color Separations

HOW DOES OFFSET PRINTING WORK?

When you prepare a project—a brochure, newsletter, poster, etc.—for commercial printing, you will deal with a print shop and possibly a service bureau.

Traditionally, a service bureau takes your prepared CorelDraw 7 files and either prints them using a high-resolution printer, giving you *camera-ready* output, or images the files onto film. If you get camera-ready output, the print shop will use a camera to shoot pictures of the output to create film.

With the advent of computers and transportable large storage media such as DAT tapes, and ZIP and JAZZ drives, many graphic artists skip the service bureau, cutting out the intermediate step of film or camera-ready output, and go straight to the print shop with disks containing their project files. Some service bureaus and print shops prefer to use the actual CorelDraw .Cdr files, while others prefer PostScript (.Ps) or encapsulated PostScript (.Eps) files.

The print shop takes any of these media—camera-ready output, film, or computer files—and uses them to make printing plates. The plates are then put on large rollers on a printing press by the *pressman*. If your project contains more than one color, the pressman uses *registration marks* to make sure all the plates are exactly aligned. He or she then runs the printing press. As the plates rotate on the rollers, they pick up a very thin coating of ink and an ink impression is transferred to the paper.

After the ink dries, the paper is trimmed and folded using *crop marks* as a guide. The *print job* is then packed and shipped to you.

How Offset Printing Works

To generate a PostScript (.Ps) file:

1. Save your project by selecting Save from the File menu or pressing Ctrl+S on the keyboard.

2. Choose Print from the File menu or press Ctrl+P. The Print dialog box will open (**Figure 1**).

3. Select the printer that you want to use. (This must be a PostScript printer.)

4. Place a check mark in the Print to file box (**Figure 17**).

5. Click OK. The Print To File dialog box will appear (**Figure 18**).

6. Move to the folder where you want to save the file.

7. Use the Save as type drop-down list to select PostScript File (*.ps) (**Figure 19**).

8. Type a name in the File name text box.

9. Click Save.

To generate an Encapsulated PostScript (.Eps) file:

1. Save your project by selecting Save from the File menu or pressing Ctrl+S.

2. Choose Print from the File menu or press Ctrl+P. The Print dialog box will open (**Figure 1**).

3. Place a check mark in the Print to file box (**Figure 17**).

4. Select the printer that you want to use. (This must be a PostScript printer.)

Figure 17. *In the Printer area of the Print dialog box, put a check mark in the box next to Print to file.*

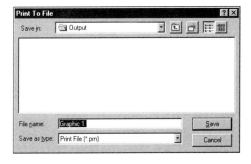

Figure 18. *Use the Print To File dialog box to set where the file will be saved, and the file's name and format extension.*

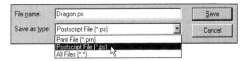

Figure 19. *Use the Save as type drop-down list to select PostScript File (*.ps), then type a name in the File name text box.*

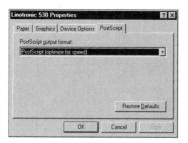

Figure 20. *Use the PostScript tab page to select the output format.*

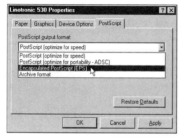

Figure 21. *Select Encapsulated PostScript (EPS) from the PostScript output format drop-down list.*

Figure 22. *Click OK in the Warning dialog box.*

Figure 23. *In the Print To File dialog box, use the Save as type drop-down list to select All Files (*.*). In the File name text box, type a name followed by .Eps.*

5. Click the Properties button. This will open the Properties dialog box for the PostScript printer you have chosen.

6. Click the PostScript tab to bring that tab page to the front (**Figure 20**). (If you don't see a PostScript tab, then you haven't selected a PostScript printer.)

7. Use the PostScript output format drop-down list to select Encapsulated PostScript (EPS) (**Figure 21**). A warning dialog box will appear telling you that Encapsulated PostScript should only be output to a file (**Figure 22**). Don't worry about this "warning." Click OK to close the dialog box.

8. Click OK to close the printer's Properties dialog box.

9. Click OK in the Print dialog box. The Print To File dialog box will open (**Figure 18**).

10. Move to the folder where you want to save the file.

11. Use the Save as type drop-down list to select All Files (*.*) (**Figure 23**).

12. In the File name text box, type the file name *followed by* .Eps (for example, MyFile.Eps). If you don't type this file extension, the file will not be saved correctly.

13. Click Save.

Generate an Encapsulated PostScript File

The Print Preview window is very helpful in that it shows you the exact area of the page that will print and gives access to all the printing options discussed in this chapter.

To open Print Preview:

If you have the Print dialog box open, click Preview (**Figure 24**).

Figure 24. *Click the Preview button in the Print dialog box.*

or

Choose Print Preview from the File menu (**Figure 25**). The Print Preview window will open (**Figure 26**).

Figure 25. *Choose Print Preview from the File menu.*

Figure 26. *The Print Preview window.*

Click here to open the Print Options dialog box Click to print Click to zoom in and out

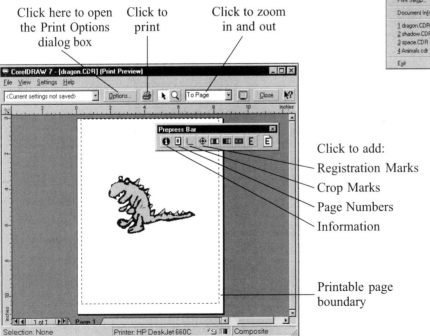

Click to add:
Registration Marks
Crop Marks
Page Numbers
Information

Printable page boundary

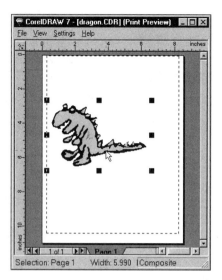

Figure 27. *Click on the drawing to select it. Eight black handles will appear around the drawing.*

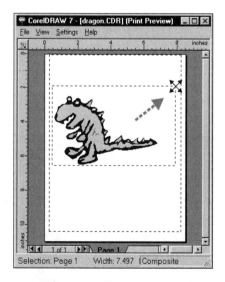

Figure 28. *As you drag, the handles will disappear and be replaced with a dashed rectangle that will grow or shrink as you drag.*

If your drawing is too large for the page or so small that it's very difficult to see and you want to print a hard copy proof, you can use the Print Preview window to dynamically scale the drawing.

To scale a drawing in Print Preview:

1. Open the Print Preview window by clicking Preview in the Print dialog box or by choosing Print Preview from the File Menu.

2. Click on the drawing. Eight black—very familiar!—handles will appear around the drawing (**Figure 27**).

3. Position the mouse over a handle, press the left mouse button, and drag the handle until the drawing is sized as you want it (**Figure 28**). The mouse pointer will change to a double-headed arrow shaped like an X. In addition, a dashed rectangle will appear around the drawing as you drag.

4. When you release the mouse, the graphic will redraw to it's new scaled size.

Tip:

- Scaling the drawing in Print Preview mode won't scale the actual drawing in your document, it will only change the size of the drawing when it's printed.

Scale the Printed Page

To position the drawing on the printed page:

1. Open the Print Preview window by clicking Preview in the Print dialog box or by choosing Print Preview from the File Menu.

2. Position the mouse over the drawing, press the left mouse button and drag the drawing to where you want it to appear on the printed page (**Figure 29**).

Tips:

- Positioning a drawing on the printed page can come in handy if your graphic is partially outside the page boundary.

- Repositioning the drawing on the printed page will not move the actual drawing in your document, it will only affect the position of the drawing on the printed page.

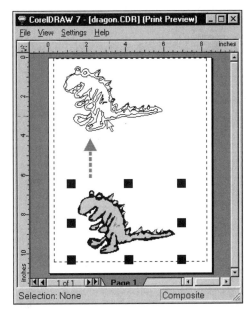

Figure 29. *Drag the drawing to position it on the printed page.*

SUMMARY

In this chapter you learned how to:

- Print documents
- Print specific pages
- Size and tile a printout
- Select different printers
- Add crop and registration marks to a printout

- Create color separations
- Generate PostScript files
- Use the Print Preview screen
- Position a drawing on the printed page

Fonts & Clipart in This Book

*B*elow is a list, divided by chapter, of the location for every font and piece of clipart used in this book. The fonts are located on CorelDraw 7 CD-ROM disk #1. The clipart that ships with CorelDraw 7 can be found on either CorelDraw 7 CD-ROM disks #2 or #3. Clipart that I have created can be found on my Website at http://www.BearHome.com/CD7/Clipart.Htm.

To add a piece of CorelDraw clipart to your document, use the Scrapbook roll-up or the Symbols roll-up. Adding clipart to a project is discussed in Chapter 16.

Chapter 1

Drop cap font: Pablo LET

Filigree: Clipart\Medieval\Sb27.Cdr

Chapter 2

Drop cap font: President

Chapter 3

Drop cap font: Galleria

Train: Clipart\Borders\Misc\Trainbdr.Cdr

Chapter 4

Drop cap font: MandarinD

Apple: Clipart\Food\Fruits\Applea.Cdr

Car: Symbols roll-up, Transportation, #74

Crown: Clipart\Spec_occ\Misc\Crown.Cdr

Football: Symbols roll-up, Sports & Hobbies, #33

Iris: Clipart\Flowers\Flowiris.Cdr

Man with top hat: Symbols roll-up,
    People, #53

Rabbits: Symbols roll-up, Animals2,
    #53; Clipart\Borders\Animals\
    Bunnies.Cdr

Sailing Ship: Clipart\Borders\Misc\
    Shipbord.Cdr

Star: Symbols roll-up, Stars1, #41

T-Rex: Clipart\Prehist\Dinosaur\
    Tyran002.Cdr

Turtles: Clipart\Borders\Animals\
    Turtle.Cdr

Chapter 5

Drop cap font: VictorianD

Dragons: Clipart\Fantasy\Dragoff.Cdr

Flag: Symbols roll-up, Festive, #134

Pow!: Clipart\Spec_occ\Misc\
    Pow_.Cdr

Snail: http://www.bearhome.com

Star border: http://www.bearhome.com

Starfish border: Clipart\Borders\
    Animals\Sea_life.Cdr

Chapter 6

Drop cap font: Algerian

Clown: Clipart\Spec_occ\Valentin\
    Valentin.Cdr

Faceted Heart: Clipart\Designs\
    Icon072.Cdr

Hearts with Arrow: Clipart\Designs\
    Hearts1.Cdr

Town: Clipart\Borders\Misc\
    Steep.Cdr

Waves: Photos\Images\Cartoons\
    Seastorm.Tif

Chapter 7

Drop cap font: Amazone BT

Flags: Clipart\Flags\Flying\
    As they appear from left to right:
    Skorea.Cdr, Canada.Cdr,
    Usa.Cdr, France.Cdr,
    Austral2.Cdr, Austria.Cdr,
    Japan.Cdr, Norway.Cdr

Chapter 8

Drop cap font: Jazz LET

Chapter 9

Drop cap font: CaslonOpnface BT

Jets: Clipart\Aircraft\Jets\C141t.Cdr;
    C141f.Cdr; C141c.Cdr;
    Airplne1.Cdr; Airplne2.Cdr

Planes: Clipart\Aircraft\Proplane\
    Ov10bf.Cdr; Ov10bt.Cdr

Chapter 10

Drop cap font: Bertram LET

Bear: Symbols roll-up, Animals1, #40

Butterfly: Symbols roll-up, Animals2,
    #57

Camel: Symbols roll-up, Animals1, #55

Elephant: Symbols roll-up, Animals1,
    #52

Frog: Symbols roll-up, Animals1, #78

Mouse: Symbols roll-up, Animals1, #74

Orcas: Clipart\Borders\Animals\
Whales.Cdr

Chapter 11

Drop cap font: ShelleyAllegro BT

Chapter 12

Drop cap font: Crazy Creatures

April: Clipart\Calendar\Months\
Month001.Cdr

Bang: Clipart\Spec_occ\Misc\Bang_.Cdr

Cyclone Crest: Clipart\Crests\Army\
38infdv1.Cdr

K: Clipart\Letters\Fun\K.Cdr

Love: www.BearHome.com

R: Clipart\Letters\Fun\R.Cdr

Ribbon: Clipart\Awards\Ribbons\
Ribb0002.Cdr

Vermont: Clipart\Travel\Misc\
Trav0097.Cdr

Chapter 13

Drop cap font: Hazel LET

Black and White Design: Clipart\
Designs\Icon032.Cdr

Cake: Clipart\Food\Desserts\Cake01.Cdr

Cat: Clipart\Animals\Pets\Cat01.Cdr

Chicken: Clipart\Birds\Landbrds\
Land0009.Cdr

Daffodil: Clipart\Flowers\Flowr006.Cdr

Finch: Clipart\Birds\Songbrds\
Finch2.Cdr

Japanese Crest: Clipart\Japan\Signs\
Crest4.Cdr

Plaque: Clipart\Awards\Plaques\
Award02.Cdr

Tulip: Clipart\Flowers\Flowr041.Cdr

Chapter 14

Drop cap font: Westwood LET

Blouse: Clipart\Fashion\Clothing\
Nwage918.Cdr

Boot: Clipart\Fashion\Clothing\
Boot.Cdr

Camel: Clipart\Africa\Art\
Camel2.Cdr

Candle: http://www.bearhome.com

Coffee Cup: Clipart\Food\Drinks\
Cofemug.Cdr

Cowboy Hat: Clipart\Fashion\Acesries\
Acses015.Cdr

Crown: Clipart\Fashion\Acesries\
Acses004.Cdr

Fish border: Clipart\Borders\Animals\
Dancfish.Cdr

Ladybug: Clipart\Insects\Flying\
Flyin011.Cdr

Lightbulb: Clipart\Home\Misc\
Litebulb2.Cdr

Party Hat: Clipart\Fashion\Acesries\
Nwage932.Cdr

Steer Head: Symbols roll-up, Animals1,
#61

TV: Clipart\Home\Electron\Tv_i.Cdr

Venus: Clipart\Fantasy\Venus.Cdr

Chapter 15

Drop cap font: Slipstream LET Plain

Bird: Symbols roll-up, Animals1, #115

Crab: Symbols roll-up, Animals1, #92

Galaxy: Clipart\Borders\Frames\ Milky.Cdr

Plane: Symbols roll-up, Transportation, #136

Rabbit: Symbols roll-up, Animals2, #53

Rocket: Clipart\Space\Rockets\ Rocket8.Cdr

Turtle: Symbols roll-up, Animals1, #72

Vulcan: Clipart\Carictre\Entertai\ Actor111.Cdr

Chapter 16

Drop cap font: Bard

Bluebird: Clipart\Birds\Songbrds\ Bluebird.Cdr

Butterfly: Photos\Objects\Animals\ Monarch.Cpt

Flowers: Photos\Photos\Flowers\ 586053.Wi

Mountain: Photos\Photos\Mountain\ 1560_26.Wi

Turtle: Photos\Objects\Animals\ Turtle.Cpt

Chapter 17

Drop cap font: Arriba Arriba LET

Bear: Clipart\Animals\Icons\ Plr_bear.Cdr

Chapter 18

Drop cap font: Charlesworth

Dragon: Clipart\Fantasy\Kkchlf11.Cdr

Electronics border: Clipart\Borders\Bars\ Hm_elect.Cdr

Appendix A

Drop cap font: ShelleyVolante BT

Fish: Clipart\Borders\Animals\ Anim0005.Cdr

Morning Glories: Clipart\Borders\ Plants\Glories.Cdr

Appendix B

Drop cap font: Zinjaro LET

Boats: Clipart\Borders\Leisure\ Fun00034.Cdr

Castle: Clipart\Borders\Leisure\ Fun00035.Cdr

The CorelDraw 7 Graphics Suite

The CorelDraw 7 Graphics Suite ships with three CD-ROM disks. On these disks are many things—from CorelDraw itself to a 3D modeling studio to photographs and clipart.

Disk 1: Programs and Fonts

In addition to CorelDraw 7, there are eleven other programs you can choose to install:

- Corel Capture—a screen capture program that lets you take "pictures" of what's on your screen.

- Corel Color Manager Wizard—sets up color profiles for computer hardware, such as your monitor, scanner, and printer, to ensure accurate color display, scanning, and printing.

- CorelDepth—this program guides you through the steps of adding three dimensional effects to your drawings.

- CorelDream 3D 7—a three dimensional modeling studio that guides you through creating 3D graphics.

- CorelMemo—this handy little program lets you create "sticky notes" while you work.

- Corel Multimedia Manager—a file management program that lets you view the contents of the font, photo, and clipart libraries on the CorelDraw 7 CD-ROMs.

- Corel Photo-Paint 7—this bitmap-based program takes over where the bitmap facilities of CorelDraw 7 leave off. You can use Photo-Paint to add super effects to your graphics and any bitmap image.

- Corel OCR-Trace—a program that helps you trace bitmap artwork to create vector drawings. It also converts type entered into the computer with a scanner into CorelDraw 7 paragraph text, allowing you to edit it in any way you choose.

- CorelScan—this program uses wizards to take you through scanning images and documents.

- CorelScript—a macro-type language that lets you create mini-programs that automate many tasks in CorelDraw and Photo-Paint.

- CorelTexture—this program helps you create interesting textures, including marble, stone, wood, and metal. You can use these custom textures as fills and backgrounds for your drawings and Web pages.

- Over 1,400 TrueType and Type 1 fonts alphabetically arranged in folders by name.

Disk 2: 3D models, photographs, and tiles

- Over 250 three dimensional models for use with CorelDream 3D 7.

- Hundreds of brush textures and tiles that are good for backgrounds and fills.

- .Tif bitmap images arranged by category in folders.

- Over 1,000 photographs saved as bitmaps and organized by category in folders. You can import them into your CorelDraw 7 projects using the Scrapbook roll-up (*see page 216*).

Disk 3: Clipart

Over 32,000 pieces of clipart that range from cars and plants to holiday and medical graphics, arranged in folders by category.

Index

Index

Index

Index

Index